OFFSHORE
SAILING

BY **DICK McCLARY**

ILLUSTRATIONS BY ANDREW SIMPSON

© Dick McClary
First Published 2011

The Royal Yachting Association
RYA House, Ensign Way, Hamble
Southampton SO31 4YA
Tel: 0844 556 9555
Fax: 0844 556 9516
E-mail: publications@rya.org.uk
Web: www.rya.org.uk
ISBN: 978-1-906435493
RYA Order Code: G87

Totally Chlorine Free | Sustainable Forests | EMAS

A CIP record of this book is available from the British Library.

Note: While all reasonable care had been taken in the preparation of this book, the publisher takes no responsibility for the use of the methods or products or contracts described in the book.

Cover Design: Velveo Design
Typesetting: Velveo Design
Proofreading and indexing: Alan Thatcher
Printed: in China through World Print
Photographs: Dick McClary

CONTENTS

FOREWORD

My first offshore sailing experience, like many South Coast sailors in the UK, was a passage across the English Channel to France at the age of ten. I clearly remember the sense of anticipation among the mostly family crew of Sibelius as we talked through the adventure ahead the night before departure! Uncle Ray had planned the passage with all the precision of a military campaign. Jack, my father and the skipper of Sibelius, was more relaxed, relying rather heavily on Ray's confident preparations.

We set out from Poole late the following morning, missing the best of the tide and immediately therefore falling outside of the original 'passage plan'. The pleasant weather lured us out until we were out of sight of land, making our 24ft yacht seem rather small. From that moment onwards the wind and seas increased in a quite alarming manner. These signals, however, 'rang no bells' among the crew. Seasickness probably affected proper decision-making, together with a misplaced, determined pride to complete the passage.

Day turned to night, magnifying the experience to a point where any sensible person was going to be fairly scared. At 10 years old, I was obviously not that sensible! Looking back at events, the dramatic storm scenes from the movie The Perfect Storm are exactly how I recall that night – although probably the wind was around force 7 or perhaps 8.

When dawn arrived off the coast, we could not identify exactly where we were and, after a period of nervous uncertainty, it became apparent that we had been swept west by the strong Channel currents, missing France altogether and perhaps fortunately coming up on the coast of Alderney. Even this rather significant error could not dampen the overwhelming relief of safe arrival and, while this clearly was not a model offshore passage, the satisfaction of its completion was tangible as we strode proudly up the hill into Braye, our French phrasebooks in our back pockets just in case.

Experiences like this can be painful, even discouraging if you are not armed with the proper knowledge. Over the years and still today, the RYA has provided the backbone of my formal training. RYA Offshore Sailing encapsulates the knowledge needed to avoid many of the pitfalls we experienced on Sibelius. It provides a framework of areas that need to be considered before heading offshore, while at the same time giving an insight into the science of sailing which I believe is a prerequisite of proper understanding. As always 'knowledge is power' and this information can also empower the reader with the confidence to head further afield. Couple this with some practical experience and steadily increasing passage distances and you and your crew can have an enjoyable and safe introduction to the freedoms and pleasures that offshore sailing can bring to those of us lucky enough to experience it.

Mike Golding

INTRODUCTION

The sea is a beguiling place. For many sailors, the more you see of it, the more you want to see. There's that first headland you sail around to find out what lies beyond, and that brings some gratification – satisfaction even – while you set about exploring the delights newly disclosed.

But not for long. For there in the distance you spot another headland, hardly more than a smudge on the horizon, hardly worth a second thought. Yet somehow you find your gaze straying to it with increasing fascination and urgency. And, before you know it, the anchor chain is clattering upwards over the bow roller and you're on your way again.

Of course, there are other forms of boating, each equally wonderful and bringing huge pleasure to multitudinous enthusiasts. But this book is for those for whom a headland is not a barrier but an irresistible temptation. In short, it's for those who are drawn offshore, perhaps even out into the oceans where the next point to be rounded lies several thousand miles away.

However, these aren't ventures that should be taken lightly. It used to be the case that navigation was the big barrier. The inexperienced sailor would first hug the coast while perfecting his or her navigational skills. Once satisfied with their growing expertise, the next step might have been a short offshore cross-Channel hop to France, relying on compass bearings and dead reckoning to track position. But to participate in the offshore and trans-ocean league called for celestial navigation – not something the novice mariner could master quickly, but in the meantime giving an opportunity for other seamanship skills to develop in parallel.

Not anymore. Electronic satellite navigation systems have made position-finding almost the least of a sailor's worries. This means that relatively inexpert crews are setting out on voyages that would have daunted their predecessors.

Fortunately, as all RYA members will know, there are country-wide training facilities, both ashore and afloat, that provide a structured means of acquiring much of the knowledge you need. But not all.

For there are also the experiences of others who have cruised far and wide and can impart the things they have learned – and learned to do well – to those who wish to do likewise. Which describes this book perfectly.

THE OFFSHORE YACHT

Offshore sailing – what do we mean by it? How does it differ from 'inshore' sailing? Or 'ocean' sailing for that matter? Well, if we can agree that inshore sailing means a coastal passage where the yacht is always within six hours of a safe haven – six hours being the 'imminent' time period in the Shipping Forecast – then it's fair to say that offshore sailing starts where inshore sailing leaves off. But the distinction between offshore and ocean sailing is rather more fuzzy. Perhaps ocean sailing could be satisfactorily described as long distance offshore sailing. After all, mid-ocean is as far offshore as you can get. But if there is a distinction, it's that ocean sailing requires an even greater degree of self-sufficiency and resourcefulness.

The Recreational Craft Directive – more about which later – has something to say about it too. It requires that a boat intended for offshore sailing shall be designed for sea conditions up to Beaufort F8 and Significant Wave Heights up to 4m. The Significant Wave Height is the average of the highest 30% of all waves and, as individual waves can be twice that, it's clear that offshore sailing is not for the faint-hearted or inadequately prepared.

With a modicum of good fortune, pretty much any reasonably sized cruising boat can make an offshore passage, even cross an ocean. And many do, but luck – an unreliable commodity with a tendency to run out altogether – isn't a sound basis upon which to plan such a venture. In challenging circumstances, and with little prospect of outside assistance, an offshore sailor must have confidence in the seaworthiness of the vessel beneath his feet. But this doesn't mean, as more than a few will have you believe, that only a heavy displacement monohull is up to the job.

An overweight, under-canvassed tub that refuses to sail much closer than a beam reach and needs half a gale to get her going at all falls a long way short of an ideal offshore cruising boat. Sailing performance that gives a boat the capacity to reach a safe haven before a storm arrives, together with the close-winded ability to beat off a lee shore to the safety of deep water, are desirable characteristics indeed.

Two correct but unhelpful answers to the question 'What's the ideal offshore cruising yacht?' include 'It depends' or 'There isn't one'. But let's turn the question around:

'What are the fundamental qualities inherent in a good offshore cruising yacht?'

An Offshore Yacht – The Fundamentals

I put this question to a group of my cruising pals. Unsurprisingly perhaps, opinions were diverse – one skipper even insisting that a plumbed-in washing machine was essential. Another felt that sailing should be closer to camping than a luxury hotel experience. Incidentally, I was closer in spirit to him than his colleague, believing that too many perceived 'home comforts' can actually detract from the sailing experience. There's a fine balance to be struck between complexity and convenience. Some years ago we were berthed in Gibraltar preparing for a passage to the Balearics. Around us, equipment chaos prevailed, the main culprits being electronic autopilots, closely followed by watermakers and refrigeration systems.

But back to our yacht club bar discussion. All the usual arguments arose – multihull v. monohull; heavy v. light displacement; sloop v. ketch; long keel v. fin keel etc. So consensus didn't come easily but, after a lengthy discussion and a few beers, we agreed that few experienced yachtsmen would argue against the following:

- Good performance under sail
- Comfortable motion under way
- Easily manageable by a small crew
- High resistance to capsize
- Sufficient internal volume for comfortable living
- Robust and easy to maintain
- Affordable to own and operate

It was clearly going to be impossible to agree any order of precedence within this list, but after another beer we did manage to condense it into four fundamental attributes:

1. Seaworthiness
2. Performance
3. Seakindliness
4. Cost

Let's look at them in turn.

Seaworthiness

Seaworthiness is a difficult concept to define precisely; many will correctly argue – your insurance company included – that it isn't just about the boat. Crew strength and experience is clearly an influencing factor, as is the extent of stores and equipment carried aboard. The whole endeavour must be 'fit for purpose'. But for the purpose of this book, I'd like to settle on a narrower definition. How about – 'a seaworthy boat is one that's capable of looking after her crew in all conditions'? You might add 'that could reasonably be anticipated within the limits of its intended cruising grounds' without detracting too much from it.

While few boats venturing offshore will ever experience extreme heavy weather unless they go looking for it, it must be said that in such conditions the greatest danger is of being rolled over by a breaking wave. The ability to resist this alarming prospect is clearly high on the list of seaworthy attributes. The height of a breaking wave capable of capsizing a boat is directly proportionate to the size of the boat, so a good big boat is always more seaworthy than a good small one. So, seaworthiness can't be described in absolute terms but, in all regards other than size, it's a function of design. Structural and watertight integrity are fundamental and, in addition to the ability to stay afloat, she must have the windward ability to manoeuvre clear of danger in heavy weather.

She must also be able to provide shelter for her crew, and to recover quickly from a knockdown. Performance, then, and comfort are part of seaworthiness and will be discussed later. Let's consider initially her resistance to capsize and the ability to recover from a knockdown. In a word – stability.

Stability

Feeling a sailboat heel under him for the first time, a novice sailor may wonder what stops it from going all the way over. Many years ago my son James asked me just that.

"It's that lump of lead in the keel," I explained.

"Why put lead in something you expect to float?" said James.

Perhaps he was onto something – I put him down as a future multihull man.

This piece of nostalgia hints at the two key ingredients to stability – ballast and hull form. Monohulls have more of the first and less of the second, and multihulls very little of the first and much of the second.

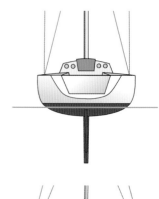

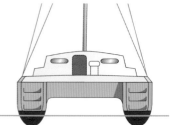

Fig. 1.1

Stability considerations fall under two further headings – static and dynamic. Static being when the boat is at rest; dynamic when under way and subject to the forces of wind and waves.

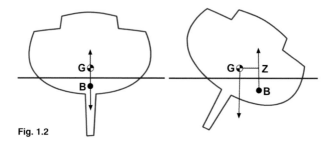

Fig. 1.2

Organisations like the RYA believe quite rightly that stability information should be available to prospective buyers and have been instrumental in getting manufacturers and designers to comply with this requirement. As a result, few sailing magazines these days fail to include stability data in the form of a GZ curve in their new boat reviews. The GZ curve illustrates the relationship between the key factors that determine the boat's static stability:

- The centre of gravity (**G**) through which gravity exerts a downward force equal to the displacement of the boat, and
- the centre of buoyancy (**B**), being the centre of the underwater volume of the boat, whose upward thrust counteracts the effect of gravity acting through, and
- the horizontal distance (GZ) between the **G** and the **B**.

The location of **G** is fixed, unlike **B** which changes as the boat heels and the immersed section changes shape. As **G** and **B** initially move apart and then converge, so the length of **Z** – the righting lever – increases and decreases. This relationship between heel angle and righting moment governs the shape of the **Z** curve and defines the boat's static stability. Thankfully it's not necessary to emulate the alarming sequence of events illustrated in fig. 1.3 to establish the curve – this is produced by calculation, these days probably via the designer's computer software.

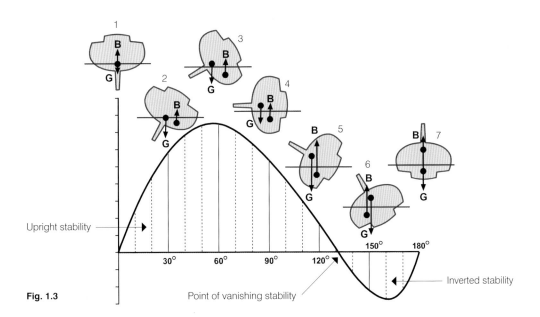

Fig. 1.3

Fig. 1.3 shows a GZ curve for our example, a typical monohull ballasted sailing yacht. Let's see what happens as the boat heels:

1. With the boat upright, **G** is in the same vertical plane as the **B** and there's no righting lever.
2. But when the boat heels to the wind, **B** will move to leeward and a righting lever is generated.
3.,4. & 5. As the boat continues to heel, the righting lever will increase to a maximum (in our example at 60° of heel) and then start diminishing until the **B** is once again in the same vertical plane as **G**. At this point the righting lever is again zero but, unlike when upright, the boat will tend to capsize if its heel angle continues to increase. This point is called the Angle of Vanishing Stability (AVS), also known as the Limit of Positive Stability (LPS), and in our example occurs at 130°. 6. Once heeled past AVS the GZ will become negative and will act as a capsizing lever rather than righting lever. 7. Unless affected by some outside force, the boat will continue to 180° of heel until the **G** and **B** are in the same vertical plane and the boat is stable again, albeit the wrong way up.

It's clear from fig. 1.1 that hull form has a significant effect on stability. When heeling, wide, flat-bottomed hulls move the **B** outboard more rapidly than narrower, 'slack bilged' hulls. In general then, the beamier the boat the greater the form stability.

At extreme angles of heel, freeboard, deck camber and coachroof design also affect stability. A good height of freeboard will improve both the maximum righting moment and the Limit of Positive Stability. A flush-decked boat or one with a very low profile coachroof will be more stable when inverted than a similar hull with a high, narrow superstructure. A low centre of gravity is always a positive contributor to stability.

Normally, the centre of gravity will be on the centreline in a properly trimmed boat, but it can be persuaded to move away from **B** to give a marked enhancement on the righting lever. Racing skippers achieve this by demanding that under-employed crew sit out to windward. Many an hour have I spent thus as race crew on other people's boats, with the toerail cutting off the blood supply to my lower limbs, frozen to the core, and with only the prospect of a beer or two back in the Tamar River Sailing Club preventing my immediate mutiny. In our boat, *Alacazam*, we can increase the righting moment when it's beneficial to do so, by using water ballast. But more about this later on.

So back to the GZ curve. For offshore yachts one of the most apparent and meaningful aspects of the curve is the AVS. However, because the force required to heel a heavy boat is more than that required to heel a lighter one, then clearly the boat's mass (or displacement) is also a significant factor. So by multiplying the righting lever by the boat's mass, the righting lever becomes a righting moment (length x mass), and the GM curve can also be considered as a Righting Moment (RM) curve. As the area under the RM curve represents the energy needed to heel the boat, then a boat of double the displacement will need twice the energy to capsize – and twice the energy to right itself following capsize. All else being equal then, heavy boats are inherently more stable than light ones.

It's worth mentioning that the oft-quoted ballast ratio can be misleading when considering stability. This ratio is a measure of the percentage of a boat's displacement taken up by ballast. Although it can give some indication of how stiff or tender a boat may be, it takes no account of the location of the ballast or of the hull shape of the boat. Two boats can have the same ballast ratios with very different righting moments. If the hulls are the same, a boat with all its ballast in a bulb at the bottom of the keel will be stiffer than a boat with a long shoal-draught keel, even though they may have the same ballast ratio.

ISO 12217

The International Standards Organisation uses both AVS and mass as its two main static stability limits in dealing with the stability of monohull ballasted sailing yachts (ISO 12217-2). The European Commission's Recreational Craft Directive (RCD) has defined sailing boats under four categories:

A. **'OCEAN'**: Designed for extended voyages where conditions may exceed winds of Beaufort F8 and Significant Wave Heights of 4m and above, and vessels largely self-sufficient.

B. **'OFFSHORE'**: Designed for offshore voyages where conditions up to and including winds of wind F8 and Significant Wave Heights up to and including 4m may be experienced.

C. **'INSHORE'**: Designed for sailing in coastal waters, large bays, estuaries, lakes and rivers where conditions up to and including wind F6 and Significant Wave Heights up to and including 2m may be experienced.

D. **'SHELTERED WATERS'**: Designed for sailing on small lakes, rivers and canals where conditions up to and including wind F4 and Significant Wave Heights up to and including 0.5m may be experienced.

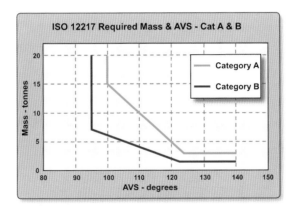

Fig. 1.4

Category A boat limits are a minimum mass of 3.0 tonnes and an AVS greater than $[130 - (2 \times \text{mass})]°$ but always equal to or greater than $100°$.

Category B boat limits are a minimum mass of 1.5 tonnes and an AVS greater than $[130 - (5 \times \text{mass})]°$ but always equal to or greater than $95°$.

Fig. 1.4 shows that a Category A boat needs to be to the right of and above the blue line and a Category B boat to the right and above the red line.

This is about as far as we can go with static stability considerations, but we need to know more. How will a boat react to a sudden gust of wind, or being hit by a strong wave?

Dynamic Stability

As we've seen, heavy displacement helps a boat's stability, but the most important factor affecting dynamic stability is the moment of inertia. This is the measure of the boat's resistance to angular acceleration. Boats rotate around three axes – rolling around the fore and aft axis; pitching about the transverse axis; yawing around the vertical axis (see page 20). It's the Roll Moment of Inertia (RMoI) that should concern us most as it's around the fore and aft axis that a boat is most likely to capsize. This is calculated by multiplying the weight of all the boat's constituent parts by the square of the distance from the boat's **G** to parts **G** – a tedious but necessary task for the designer. The squared term means that the distance of heavy items from **G** greatly affects the RMoI, and the greater RMoI the less the boat will react to a gust of wind, or a large wave. So boats with their ballast deep in their keels, their fuel and water tanks as far outboard as possible, and long heavy masts will have greater RMoIs and will be more dynamically stable as a result. Such boats will have long roll periods and will be highly resistant to rapid changes in heel angle.

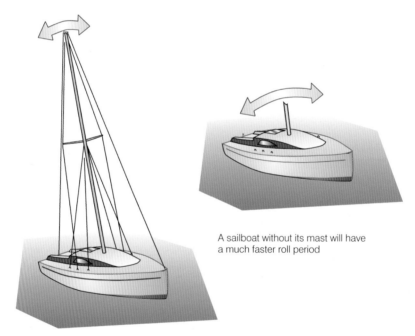

A sailboat without its mast will have a much faster roll period

Fig. 1.5

This will be very apparent to a crew unfortunate enough to have lost their rig, as this item is the boat's greatest contributor to the moment of inertia. Without it, the boat's roll period will be very quick and snappy, and the probability of capsize much higher.

Makers of grandfather clocks had cause to be grateful for the effects of the rotational moment of inertia. They used it to govern the rate of gain, or loss, of their creations. To correct a 'slow' clock, the pendulum would be shortened slightly, thereby reducing the distance to the neutral axis. This decreased the period of oscillation – it would swing faster – and speed up the clock's mechanism. Conversely, for a clock that gained, the pendulum would be increased in length to create the opposite effect. The principal reason for using pendulums in clocks was that, for a given length, the period of oscillation remains constant, irrespective of the amplitude. And so it is with a boat; if she's rolling gently at anchor, or from gunwale to gunwale in a seaway, the roll period will be the same.

STIX

The development of STIX (**ST**ability Inde**X**) by an ISO working group went some way further to address the dynamic issue. STIX, a numerical index which scores a boat's stability on a scale of 1 to 100, is a function of a number of safety and stability related features, i.e.:

- Length on deck
- Ability to withstand a capsize by considering the area under the GZ curve
- Recovery from inversion by considering AVS and mass
- Recovery from knockdown by overcoming water in the sails
- Displacement/Length Ratio giving credit for a heavy displacement for a given length
- Beam/Displacement Factor recognizing problems associated with topside flare and excessive beam
- Wind moment representing the risk of flooding due to a gust
- The risk of down-flooding in a broach or knockdown

STIX scores generally fall in the range 5 to 50 and are applied in addition to the above limits on mass and AVS, i.e.:

Category A boats: equal to or greater than 32

Category B boats: equal to or greater than 23

Since June 1998 all new recreational boats sold in the European Community have been required by law to have undergone a stability assessment with the preferred method being the application of ISO 12217. This means that all but a very small number of new monohull ballasted sailing boats sold in the EU will have had a GZ/RM curve generated, their displacement and AVS determined and a STIX calculated. For further information, see G23 RYA Stability & Buoyancy.

RYA code G23

Performance

There's no real argument in favour of a slow boat – after all, you can sail a quick boat slowly, but you can't sail a slow boat quickly. The advantages of sailing quickly are clear, and were brought home to me during a passage from Portugal to Madeira, a distance of 480-odd nautical miles. The internet forecast was for favourable conditions so we planned on a passage time of 80 hours at our usual 6 knots boat speed. We left Portimão shortly after dawn along with another yacht, agreeing to keep in touch on the VHF and planning to arrive together around midday on the fourth day. She was about the same length overall as us, but with pretty little overhangs at each end. 250NM out our rather clunky first-generation GPS told us we were at 0.00°N and 0.00°W and no amount of tapping and tweaking at either the instrument or the antenna end would persuade it to say otherwise. The NAVTEX and the barometer were now suggesting that the internet forecast ashore was on the optimistic side, and we could expect things to get worse, which they rapidly did. I remember getting one sunsight in before the sun became but a lighter patch in a dark sky and the true horizon was lost in a series of approaching wave crests. Now reduced to dead reckoning, and with the other boat left astern and out of VHF range, I was concerned that we may be on our Atlantic crossing a little earlier than anticipated. Fortunately the island of Porto Santo appeared pretty much where it should have done and, in the worsening conditions, we ducked into the sheltered harbour, much relieved. But the point of this little tale is that the other, slower boat spent a further two nights at sea, hove-to in awful conditions. We met them ashore sometime later – Mary and I looking for a new GPS and our friends trying to find a sailmaker. Our conversation centred around what a difference a knot or two makes.

And, over a long passage, a knot makes a great deal of difference. The classic passage from the Canary Islands to the West Indies, taking in the initial dogleg south to pick up the trade winds, is about 3,000NM. At 6 knots our planned voyage from Tenerifé to Guadeloupe would take around 21 days, at 7 knots 18 days but at 5 knots 25 days. So, just one knot of extra speed makes 3 days' difference on this passage, or a day for every 1,000NM sailed. We took 18 days, not bad for a 38ft (11.6m) cruiser, but Mary challenged the whole argument for fast cruising as, having enjoyed it so much, I didn't want to stop.

Speed/Length Ratio

So what makes one boat quicker than another? This question was pondered long and hard by William Froude (1810–1869). Froude, a civil engineer and colleague of Isambard Kingdom Brunel, had a special fascination with the sea and ships. Funded by the Admiralty, he built a tank testing facility at Torquay, where he experimented with various model hull forms. As an early expert in model analysis he was well acquainted with the 'law of mechanical similitude', which demonstrates among other things that there are few linear relationships in hull design.

Consider your hull as a matchbox – not wonderfully efficient hydrodynamically, but stick with it for a moment. Dissatisfied with the constraints of matchbox living, you decide to double its size. You add another matchbox ahead to double its length, two alongside to double its beam and four on top to double its draught. Now wetted area has increased by four, volume and displacement by eight and stability – as the product of its mass and acceleration – has increased sixteenfold. So by doubling a hull's dimensions, wetted area is squared, displacement is cubed and stability increases by the power of four.

With this knowledge and that gained by carefully measuring applied force and resultant movement, Froude was able both to calculate and demonstrate that a relationship existed between hull speed and waterline length – that relationship being known and described in the metric world as 'Froude Numbers'. However, most of us more accustomed to units of feet and knots are probably more familiar with the Froude Number's close relation – the Speed/Length Ratio. This is expressed as:

> S/L Ratio = $V/\sqrt{L}$
>
> Where V is the hull speed in knots, and
>
> L is the waterline length in feet

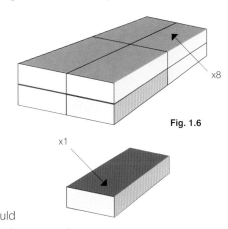

Fig. 1.6

This discovery enabled Froude to compare the performance of boats of different length. For example, a 25ft sail boat moving at 5 knots would have the same S/L Ratio as a 100ft patrol boat steaming along at 10 knots, and consequently both would develop the same resistance per ton of displacement at those speeds.

For Froude's models, having no rig above the waterline to create windage, this resistance was caused by two principal factors:

- Drag
- Wavemaking resistance

Drag

Any boat under way will experience drag, defined as the net force opposing forward movement due to the pressure and shear forces acting on the surface of the hull. It's a function of underwater shape and skin friction. Sadly, the finer points of hydrodynamic design are well beyond my grasp, but clearly the matchbox described above would create more drag than a lozenge shape of similar size. Skin friction is created by surface roughness, and at low speeds is the major drag component – as much as 65% at an S/L Ratio of 1.0, reducing to about 10% at an S/L Ratio of 1.5. And clearly the more 'skin', or wetted area, the greater the total frictional resistance. This is brutally driven home to the heavy-displacement chaps at anti-fouling time, when they find they have a lot more scrubbing to do than their light-displacement colleagues and need to dig deeper into their pockets for the required quantity of paint.

But it's not just the marine flora and fauna that do the damage. Pitted anti-fouling and protruding skin fittings all conspire to slow us up. Each protrusion disturbs laminar flow and creates a turbulent volume of water, rapidly changing its velocity and pressure and spinning off eddies and vortices. Nature doesn't like pressure difference, even less a vacuum, and always seeks to level things out. The energy required to re-establish laminar flow downstream of the protrusion is drawn from the forward momentum of the boat, which slows down as a consequence. Incidentally, we sailors should be very grateful that nature exhibits the same tendency in the atmosphere, as without it there'd be no wind.

Wavemaking Resistance

Not to be confused with the resistance experienced when punching through wind-blown waves, this is the energy loss due to the wavemaking characteristics of the boat itself.

As a boat moves ahead, the water is parted to allow the hull to move through it. A transverse bow wave forms at the forward end of the hull and a similar wave is created at the stern. The back of the bow wave forms a trough, and then a second wave that moves aft as speed increases. Eventually, that second wave will have moved right aft where it combines and reinforces the stern wave. At this point, the boat is said to have reached 'hull speed' and for many this is as quick as it can ever be expected to sail.

Froude observed that at this point, where the bow is supported by the bow wave and the stern by the stern wave, the resistance to greater speed is significantly increased. It's not difficult to see why. If the stern wave was to move further aft, the stern would drop into the trough. To go any quicker the boat would have to climb over the bow wave – an uphill struggle in every sense and this occurs at an S/L Ratio of 1.34.

The hull speed on any non-planing vessel can be found by transposing the S/L Ratio formula to:

Hull speed (knots) = LWL (in feet) x 1.34

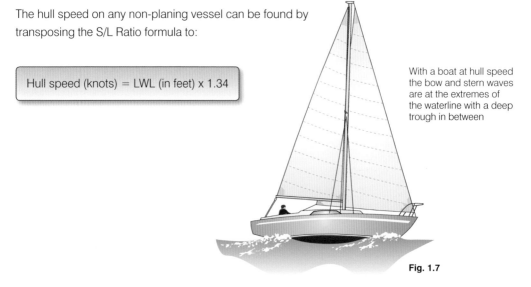

With a boat at hull speed the bow and stern waves are at the extremes of the waterline with a deep trough in between

Fig. 1.7

So, predictably, the longer the waterline, the greater the hull speed.

But clearly some boats can exceed hull speed since, if this were a limiting factor, a Laser 470 dinghy shouldn't be able to exceed 3.5 knots – which of course they do. It's all about power – sail area in a yacht and horsepower in a motorboat. We cruisers can experience this heady sensation in our inflatable tenders. Leaving the dock we gradually wind back the throttle until we're cheerfully chugging along at hull speed. A further twist of the throttle gets us to a bow-up, stern-down attitude, but we go no faster and use more fuel. If the outboard motor is powerful enough, another twist of the throttle will level the boat out as the bow wave travels under the hull, releasing us to zip across the water at a clip.

Now we can reduce power to something just above that needed to maintain hull speed and still stay on the plane. This happy state of affairs comes to an end when the throttle is closed; the boat slows, the bow wave catches us up, slops over the transom, and soaks the groceries.

Some cruising boats are capable of exceeding hull speed, and a most desirable ability it is too in my view. Provided, that is, the other previously listed attributes aren't too compromised as a result.

Hull speed can only be achieved if the boat carries sufficient sail area to develop the requisite power, and this is more for a heavy-displacement boat than it is for one of lighter displacement. We'll be dealing with what's known as the 'Sail Area/Displacement Ratio' very shortly.

Prismatic Coefficient

Wavemaking resistance isn't only a function of length. The shapes of the immersed fore and aft hull sections have an influence upon it too. What is actually crucial here is the rate of change of the cross-sectional areas of the hull. A hull which changes slowly will generate less wavemaking resistance than a hull with a rapid rate of change. This is where the prismatic coefficient comes in – it's a measure of how quickly the cross-sectional area changes or, in sailing parlance, of how full or fine the ends are.

The prismatic coefficient is defined as 'the ratio of the immersed volume to the volume of a prism with its length equal to the waterline length and cross-sectional area equal to the maximum cross-sectional area', i.e.:

Prismatic Coefficient $(C_p) = V/_{AL(max)}$

Where:

V is the immersed volume of the hull in ft^3

A is the maximum cross-sectional area in ft^2

L is the waterline length in feet

The prismatic coefficient thus indicates the longitudinal distribution of the underwater volume of a yacht's hull – a low (fine) prismatic coefficient indicates a hull with fine ends. A large (full) prismatic coefficient indicates a hull with relatively full ends.

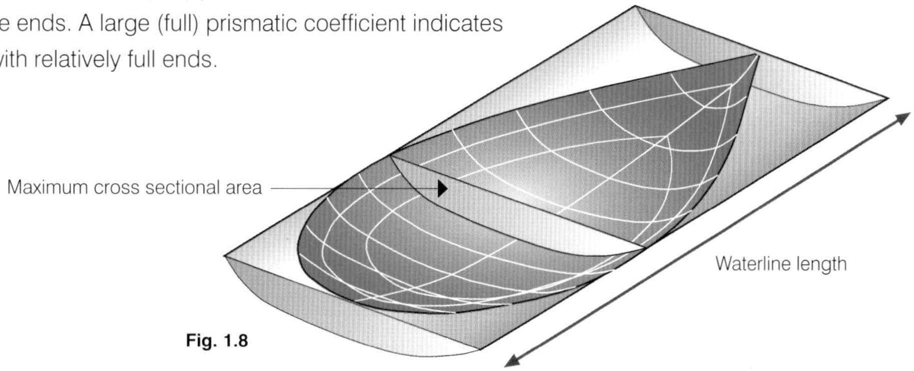

Maximum cross sectional area

Waterline length

Fig. 1.8

But it doesn't end there. The American Admiral David W. Taylor discovered while working on warship design during the First World War that, for every Speed/Length Ratio, there's an optimum prismatic coefficient, as follows:

Speed/Length Ratio	Prismatic Coefficient (Cp)
1.0 and below	.525 (fine)
1.1	.54
1.2	.58
1.3	.62
1.4	.64
1.5	.66
1.6	.68
1.7	.69
1.8 and above	.70 (full)

So for a displacement boat sailing at its maximum S/L Ratio of 1.34, the optimum Cp is 0.63. But in light conditions most boats won't achieve anything like their hull speed, and so would be punished in these conditions by a Cp optimised for hull speed. And herein lays the designer's dilemma, as his creation will sometimes be nudging along gently in light airs and at others blasting along at hull speed or beyond. Knowledge of the predominating conditions in the area that the boat is to be sailed will help him select the Cp. It's something of a black art, based on technical knowledge and empirical guesswork – and having made his decision, he's likely to keep it very close to his chest.

Displacement and Sail Area

Displacement is defined as the volume of water displaced by a boat afloat. Like speed, it doesn't mean much unless compared to length, so the following formula is used to compare the relative heaviness of boats no matter what their size:

Displacement/Length Ratio $= D/(0.01L)^3$

Where:

D is the displacement in tons

(1 ton = 2,240lb)

L is the waterline length in feet

An ultra-light racing yacht may have a D/L Ratio of 100 or so; a light cruiser/racer would be around 200; a medium displacement cruiser would be around 300, while a Colin Archer-type heavy-displacement cruiser may boast a D/L ratio of 400+.

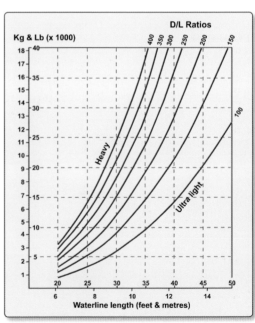

As immersed volume and displacement are proportional, a heavy-displacement yacht will have to heave aside a greater mass of water than its light-displacement cousin, or put another way, the lower D/L Ratio vessel will have a lower resistance to forward motion than the higher D/L ratio vessel and will be quicker as a result. That's a long-winded way of saying that the greater the mass, the greater the power required to shift it. That power is of course derived from the force of the wind acting upon the sails, and the greater the sail area the greater the power produced for a given wind strength. Clearly then, performance is a function of both power and weight, or sail area and displacement, and is expressed as:

Sail Area/Displacement Ratio = $SA/(DISPL)^{.667}$

Where SA is sail area in ft^2, and

DISP is displacement in ft^3 (ie $^{lbf}/_{64}$)

Sail Area/Displacement ratios range from around 14 for a lightly canvassed motor-sailer to 20 or so for an ocean racer.

So to summarise, the criteria associated with good performance under sail are:

- Waterline length: the longer the better, as wavemaking resistance is inversely proportional to waterline length.
- Wetted area: the less the better, particularly in areas where light airs prevail, as drag is directly proportional to wetted area.
- Displacement: the lower the better, as the power requirement is directly proportional to displacement. Provided, of course, that light displacement doesn't come at the cost of structural integrity.
- Sail area: the more the better, within reason, as power production is directly proportional to sail area. Having to reef early is much less frustrating than wishing you had an extra metre or so on the mast when the wind falls away.

But performance in an offshore cruising boat isn't just about speed. While, as part of the deal for getting their hands on the silverware, a racing crew will cheerfully accept the high degree of attentiveness needed to keep a twitchy racing machine on her feet, a cruising sailor most definitely won't. For us, a degree of speed will be readily sacrificed for a boat that's easy on the helm, and which rewards its crew with a gentler motion and more comfortable ride.

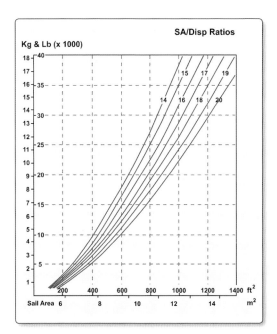

Seakindliness

Nothing endears a boat more to its crew than the way in which it handles. For a shorthanded crew – as many offshore cruisers are – good handling characteristics are paramount. Poor sail trim contributes greatly to poor handling, of course, but some boats defy all attempts to get them to handle in an acceptable manner. Such tiresome boats, despite any other wonderful attributes they may have, are the antithesis of a good offshore cruising boat. The offshore crew has a right to expect three principal qualities:

- A boat that's easy on the helm and can be trimmed to provide a small degree of weather helm. Not one that heels alarmingly and gripes up in every gust, leaving the helmsman with no option but to dump the main in a hurry.
- Good directional stability. A boat that can be left to sail herself for a few moments while the helmsman puts the kettle on is a great boon. Such a boat will respond well to a windvane self-steering system or draw the minimum current from an autopilot.
- Responsive to the helm under both sail and power. A boat should be capable of tacking up a narrow channel or a river to her mooring, and wriggling in and out of tight marina berths under power.

But not only must she handle well, she must also have a comfortable easy motion under way.

As we saw earlier when discussing stability, a boat rotates around three axes. The combined effect of this movement together with forward motion, and taken as the locus of a single point, is a distorted helix. It is not surprising then, that some of us can feel a little queasy at times. It's not only the magnitude of these movements that causes the problem – much of the discomfort is caused by the angular rate of change.

Fig. 1.9

Take the roll motion for example, which probably has the most profound effect on crew comfort and fatigue. It's not just the extent of the roll angle, but the period of the roll and the 'jerkiness' experienced at the ends of the roll. This jerkiness, the roll acceleration, is the force that's likely to throw you off balance and is the primary culprit in inducing seasickness. As we saw earlier, boats with a high Roll Moment of Inertia will benefit from a slow roll, with low levels of acceleration, and be more comfortable than their lighter but quicker counterparts.

Size, of course, has much going for it as far as seakindliness is concerned, as the bigger the boat the less it will leap about.

Ted Brewer, a well-respected American designer, in an attempt to compare the predicted motion of one boat against that of another, drafted a formula – the 'Comfort Ratio', i.e.:

$$CR = Displacement/[65 \times (0.7 \times \text{waterline length} + 0.3 \times \text{length overall}) \times beam^{1.333}]$$

Displacement in lbs, length and beam in feet.

This formula favours heavier, narrow-beamed boats with longish overhangs – it's an inescapable fact that when the sea gets up a beamy, flat-bottomed, light-displacement boat will be less comfortable than a narrow, deep-hulled, heavy one.

Comfort Ratios will range from around 10 for a light-displacement cruiser to 60-odd for a heavy-displacement Colin Archer type. So if comfort means everything to you then 'heavy' is the way to go, but you'll lose out on performance. This concept of trade-off and compromise – optioneering – is what the yacht designer's art is all about. You just can't have it all, although the deeper your pocket the closer to it you can get.

Cost

Price, cost, value and budget – the commercial conundrum that we all have to wrestle with. Price is the easy bit; that's what you can expect to pay according to what's on the tag. Cost is what you incur; the sum of all those price tags together with other fees and charges associated with owning just about anything. Cost comes in two forms – anticipated and out-turn – and it's the difference between the two that can blow your budget out of the water. Value for money is what we must look for, but sadly this is rarely associated with a low price. More often than not a low-price item, particularly in the marine environment, will require early repair or replacement. A wise old salt once told me that 'only a very wealthy man can afford to buy cheap'.

It's a fact that in recent years the price of new boats has fallen to the extent that a coastal cruiser can be purchased for little more than the price of a decent family car. Much of the saving can be attributed to increasingly efficient production techniques, and through moving production to cheaper labour-cost areas in Eastern Europe and Asia. In some cases, good design and quality control has been sacrificed on the altar of economic pressure. Sadly, the sea makes no allowance for such shortcomings, and boats and their crews have suffered badly in conditions that they should have endured.

With one new production yacht looking much like another, appearance can be no guide to quality. A prospective buyer would be wise to take heed of the old adage 'all that glitters is not gold' and to look behind the glitz and glamour.

The true value of a yacht can be seen in the quality of the gear selected by its manufacturer and the care and robustness with which they've been fitted. Inspection of a lower-cost yacht is likely to reveal a general insufficiency of cleats and handholds, grabrails and stanchions without proper backing plates, inadequate non-slip surfacing to decks and cockpits, and under-specified winches and deck gear, all of which could conspire to spoil your day.

Displacement Types

We've seen that displacement has a significant influence on stability, performance and comfort. Now let's turn it around and look at four distinct displacement categories and see the strengths and weaknesses that each one has to offer.

Heavy Displacement

With a Displacement/Length Ratio of 400+, this older style of boat has fewer devotees these days, though for passionate traditionalists it's de rigueur. Boats of this type will have a full (or long) keel, which will bring with it some benefits – and some significant limitations.

In light winds, a boat of this type will sail slowly – if at all – due to the drag caused by its high wetted area and the power required to shift its massive weight. It will only just be getting into its stride when other more moderate types are taking in reefs.

Apart from its contribution towards a boat's stability the next most important function of a keel is to resist leeway. Unfortunately, long, low-aspect ratio keels aren't very good at this so they must make up in area what they lack in efficiency.

To counteract the drag caused by the surface area more sail area is required, so to enable the boat to stand up more ballast is needed, which is why long-keelers need to be heavy and why they are often underpowered.

My first 'proper' cruising boat (a Nicholson 32, *Jalingo II*) was a craft of this type. *Jalingo's* long keel kept her tracking as if on rails, but it was important to keep plenty of way on to get her through the wind when a tack was called for. Her motion under way was sedate, but as comfortable as you could get for a boat of this size. Her vee'd forward sections gave a soft ride but she did show a tendency to bury her bows, making her a little wet at times.

But my enthusiasm for her excellent directional stability at sea largely evaporated during close-quarters manoeuvring. She was a nightmare in a marina, where going astern with any degree of directional certainty was well nigh impossible. Try launching a paper dart backwards and you will see exactly why this happens.

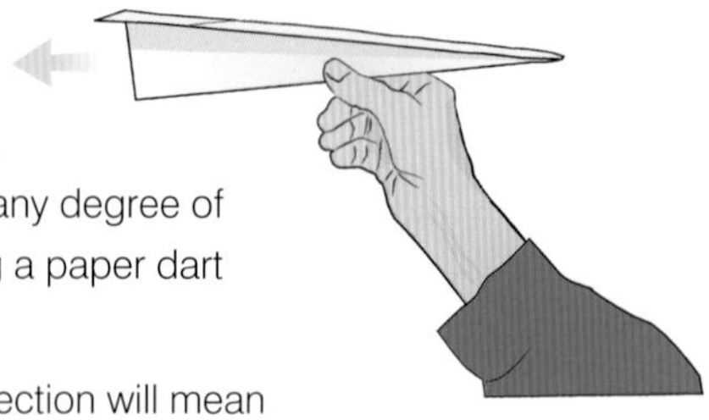

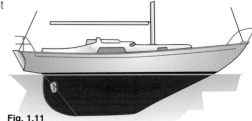

Fig. 1.10

When heeled, the general symmetry of the immersed hull section will mean they should remain well balanced at high heel angles, but the barn-door proportions of their unbalanced rudders and the fact that they are often raked off the vertical make them heavy on the helm at all times.

Fig. 1.11

With their shallow draught, protected propeller and rudder these boats will take the ground well, and should breeze over floating ropes and nets without a problem. Their high load-carrying capacity will be greatly appreciated by live-aboard sailors, which together with their other attributes will probably make them best suited for those sailors with ambitions to spend much of their time offshore in remote areas of the world. But for those of us who are more inclined to spend our time island-hopping in the Caribbean and Mediterranean, and cruising offshore in Europe and the USA, their sluggish performance will make them less attractive.

Medium Displacement

This is a natural development of the heavy-displacement craft, with a moderate-length fin keel and a separate rudder which is either transom-hung or supported on a skeg. On GRP boats, the fin keel may be part of the hull moulding and have its ballast encapsulated within. This avoids the need for keel bolts, and the corrosion and security issues often associated with them.

Although still on the heavy side by modern standards, with a D/L Ratio of around 300, this type remains a firm favourite with many long-distance cruisers. Performance, while not of the 'ocean greyhound' nature, should be adequate in most conditions and, owing to the separation of keel and rudder, manoeuvrability under both power and sail will be much improved.

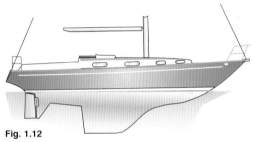

Fig. 1.12

For a given Sail Area/Displacement Ratio her sail area will be less than for the heavy-displacement type, making her easy to handle for a small crew. Directional stability and balance will be dependent on the quality of the design, and there's no reason why both shouldn't be excellent.

Light Displacement

Driven partially by the need for economy in a competitive market – lighter means less material – and an increasing demand for better performance, more and more yachts are falling into this category. Typically with a D/L Ratio of around 200, a modern light-displacement production boat – often dubbed a 'cruiser/racer' – will sport a medium-aspect ratio fin keel.

The rudder will be either transom hung, or be supported by a short skeg, or be a cantilevered spade type. The underwater shape will be dinghy-like, with minimal overhangs at bow and stern to maximise waterline length.

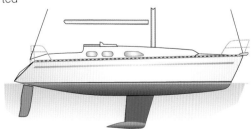

Fig. 1.13

A lot of ballast is clearly not an option for a light-displacement boat as so much of its stability is gained through increased beam, which means that when excessively heeled the asymmetry of the immersed hull sections coupled with the broad beam carried well aft can make them hard on the helm. Much is to be gained by reefing these boats early and sailing them fairly flat. Performance will be brisk in nearly all conditions, especially off the wind, when hull speed may well be exceeded. Sailing hard on the wind in vigorous conditions will be less comfortable than in a heavier displacement craft. The flatter forward sections can tend to pound, and the ride is likely to be on the lively side.

Apart from beating to windward in heavy weather they are a delight to sail, pointing high and tacking through the wind with ease – and passage times shouldn't be disappointing.

Handling under power, both ahead and astern, will be good. Except, that is, when at low speed in a crosswind. This was brought home to me during our early days with *Alacazam*, when motoring astern out of a marina berth in Leixões (approximately pronounced 'Layshoyns') in Portugal. The wind was blowing from the direction I wanted to go, but as soon as I cleared the berth and put the helm over the wind blew the bow off so I was pointing at the next berth down. Someone once said that the height of stupidity is doing the same thing over and over again, and expecting a different result. I thought of this as I found myself zig-zagging sideways down a cul de sac, greeting a series of worried-looking crews on the way. Fortunately *Alacazam* steers astern almost as well as ahead so the obvious solution – which fortunately occurred to me before we reached the wall at the end – was to let the bow blow around and motor out astern, past my visibly relieved audience, until there was enough room to turn. Another lesson learned.

The load-carrying capacity of smaller light-displacement boats can be a concern. Clearly, if you load, say, 1,500lb of stores and equipment on a 25ft boat with a D/L Ratio of 200 it will have a greater effect than if you loaded the same amount onto a 40-footer of the same D/L Ratio. The 25 footer's D/L Ratio would increase to 242 and the 40-footer's to 210 – obviously a more performance-sapping penalty for the smaller boat.

Ultra-Light Displacement

These ultra-light displacement boats (ULDBs) are probably at least one step too far for the vast majority of offshore cruising sailors. Sharing many of the characteristics of the previous category but more so, these will be beamier, lighter and deeper draughted. Keels will be high-aspect ratio and of such depth to prevent anchoring anywhere near the beach.

Performance in the right conditions, however, will be awesome. These types will readily unstick themselves from the limitations of hull speed and plane like dinghies, and it should come as no surprise that Ted Brewer's comfort ratio isn't high on the list of design considerations.

To build such a light boat while making her sufficiently strong calls for exotic materials and hi-tech building techniques, both of which come with a high price; so much so that cruising versions are generally owned by people with Lamborghinis, and backyards the size of Regent's Park.

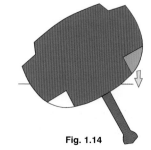

Fig. 1.14

Optimum performance, handling and comfort can't all be found at the same place on the sliding scale of displacement. Displacement, or more accurately the D/L Ratio, has a greater influence on the way in which a boat behaves in a given set of conditions than any other parameter, and should be a crucial consideration for a prospective buyer. While boats at the heavy end will have a more comfortable motion, passage times will be slower and handling more cumbersome. At the other end, the blistering performance of a ULDB will shake your fillings loose. Somewhere though, between these two extremes, lies your ideal compromise.

Water Ballast

Water ballast in a cruising boat? Not a concept the traditionalists are likely to accept unreservedly, but I think it deserves a serious look. In fact, I've already looked – which is why *Alacazam* had ballast tanks built into her wood-epoxy hull from the start. She's not dependent on this for stability – it just supplements the permanent ballast in the keel bulb with additional weight to windward

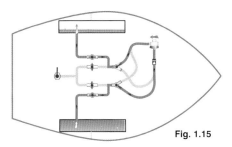

Fig. 1.15

when required. The water is carried in a tank on each side at the extremity of the waterline beam, each capable of being independently filled and drained by two 12v electric pumps. This is well below the point of maximum beam, but has the following effect:

- The boat's CG is no longer on the centreline as in fig. 1.3, but transferred outboard
- As the boat heels, the righting moment increases due to the extended horizontal distance between the centre of buoyancy of the hull and the centre of gravity of the water ballast
- The RMoI is significantly increased in terms of both pitch and roll
- If caught with the water ballast on the wrong tack, the converse of the above applies such that the heel to leeward is not dramatically affected

Initially, the cruising man in me was reluctant to forego the increased freshwater capacity that the ballast tanks could provide, so they were used to supplement the standard water tanks located close to, and either side of, the centreline. However, after lugging over 1,000lbs of this additional water all the way across the Atlantic without using any of it, I converted it to a seawater system.

Now I can get rid of it and replace it as required, and think of it as adjustable displacement. Tacking is done by opening a couple of simple valves and switching on the appropriate transfer pump. The boat's then tacked in the normal way, and when the transfer is complete, the valves are closed and the pumps switched off.

Hard on the wind, with both windward tanks full, *Alacazam* heels about 6° less for the same sail area and wind strength than she otherwise would, and sails quicker as a consequence. The concentration of outboard weight in the centre section of the boat noticeably improves the fore-and-aft stability and, coupled with less heel, reduces pitch and roll appreciably, the increased displacement bearing out Ted Brewer's Comfort Ratio.

As the wind moves aft, the forward tank is drained and when well off the wind both tanks are drained. Of course, in a short-tacking situation, the valve-turning and pump-switching involved in swapping the water from one side to the other requires a lot more rushing about than I'm accustomed to, so we only use the water ballast on long offshore tacks.

The downside is that the tanks and the plumbing take up space that could otherwise be used for stowage, but there's no doubt that a moderate degree of water ballast in a light-ish displacement cruising yacht can improve both her performance and crew comfort.

Multihulls

Multihulls are becoming increasingly popular for offshore cruising and it's not difficult to understand why:

- Shallow draught enables them to go where most monohulls can't.
- Relying almost entirely on form stability, their SA/DISP Ratio is high, giving good performance, particularly off the wind.
- Heeling is minimal. Sailing on the level is very attractive to many people.

It's usually catamarans that come to mind when we think of multihulls, but for a small crew that enjoy sailing really fast and can accept Spartan living conditions, a trimaran may well be their first choice. Unlike a catamaran, where the accommodation is built into both hulls and the central structure, living space on a trimaran is restricted to the centre hull, which has less volume than a monohull of similar length.

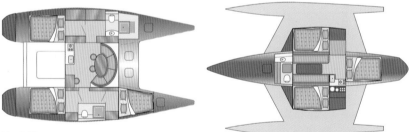

Fig. 1.16

Therein lies the problem with a number of production catamarans. The temptation is to maximise accommodation – and hence the appeal to the charter market – to the detriment of everything else. Four separate cabins, each with a double berth, is the norm in a 38-footer designed for chartering. In these boats, the bridgedeck is often set low to provide standing headroom in the saloon, when it would be better set higher to enable waves to pass unhindered beneath it. The resultant noise and slamming is not something that can be easily ignored. The windage of these bungalow-proportioned types has led to the catamaran's reputation as a poor windward performer, and this is particularly so when reefed down in heavy weather.

Like all light-displacement craft, overloading will decrease the SA/DISP Ratio and spoil the performance. Consequently, small high-volume cats, when loaded with the equipment for offshore cruising, can become dogs. And it's for this reason that, in my opinion, offshore cruising catamarans only begin to make sense at around 45 feet.

On the wind, owing to their minimal draught, catamarans can make considerable leeway. Most have vestigial keels to resist this tendency, but those designed really to tramp on have daggerboards.

At sea, their inability to absorb the small variations in the wind by heeling gives them a peculiar, lurching movement which can be a bit disconcerting until you get used to it. Also, the rapid variations in speed and the effects these have on the apparent wind direction mean that windvane self-steering systems find it very difficult to keep multihulls on a straight course.

However, a properly designed catamaran from the board of a designer unconstrained by the requirements of the charter market can make a fine offshore cruising boat. In reasonable conditions a well-sailed craft of this type can often arrive at an upwind destination earlier than a monohull of similar length, any inferior pointing ability having been compensated for by a higher speed through the water and resulting VMG (Velocity Made Good).

Under power, their manoeuvrability can be remarkable. If they have an engine in each hull, putting one astern and the other ahead will turn a catamaran in its own length with ease – a redeeming feature in a marina, where you're likely to attract a hefty surcharge for a berth. For more information see G92 RYA Multihull Handbook for Cruisers.

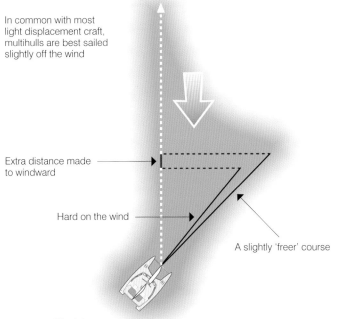

In common with most light displacement craft, multihulls are best sailed slightly off the wind

Extra distance made to windward

Hard on the wind

A slightly 'freer' course

RYA code G92

Fig. 1.17

Draught

Envy is reputed to be a sin, but crews of deep-keeled monohulls rolling around on the outer edge of an anchorage can be forgiven for casting envious glances towards the shallow-draught craft laying in sublime tranquility closer in. While it's true that a deep-fin keel is the most efficient of all in terms of windward ability combined with the least frictional resistance, many anchorages will be opened up to those who opt for a shallow-draught alternative, accepting the perceptible loss to windward. Another benefit with the longer shallow-fin keel is the increased security to be had when lying alongside a wall, or laid-up ashore in a cradle.

Bulbs, Wings and Things

One way to reduce draught while minimising the effect on stability is to provide additional ballast in the form of a lead bulb on the bottom of the keel. Variations on this theme include torpedoes, the Scheel keel and the wing keel. Properly designed 'torpedoes' meet this requirement and providing they don't project forward of the keel's leading edge – where they'll collect pick-up lines, discarded fishing nets and other assorted flotsam and jetsam – are a good solution for offshore yachts.

The Scheel keel, invented by the American designer Henry A. Scheel, is said to create additional lift through the converse sections on top of the bulb, and appears on several highly regarded offshore designs.

Wing keels develop this principle further, but share the same propensity as the forward-projecting torpedo for collecting unwanted hangers-on. Wings increase wetted area, and hence drag, but as well as producing more hydrodynamic lift they do provide a degree of 'damping' in a rolling anchorage. You'll need to support the boat in slings to anti-foul the underside of the wing, or alternatively employ a diver to scrub it clean at regular intervals.

Lifting Keels

These types rely on ropes and pulleys, or hydraulic rams in some cases, to retract a steel centreplate into a keel housing. Some types operate vertically and others pivot around a pin at the forward end. In some designs a ballast stub keel is retained, which contains the keel housing. Others have no stub keel at all and all of the keel housing projects into the boat to some degree, usually to the detriment of the accommodation. When all goes well a lifting keel would seem the ideal solution to provide deep draught offshore and shoal draught when navigating in shallow waters.

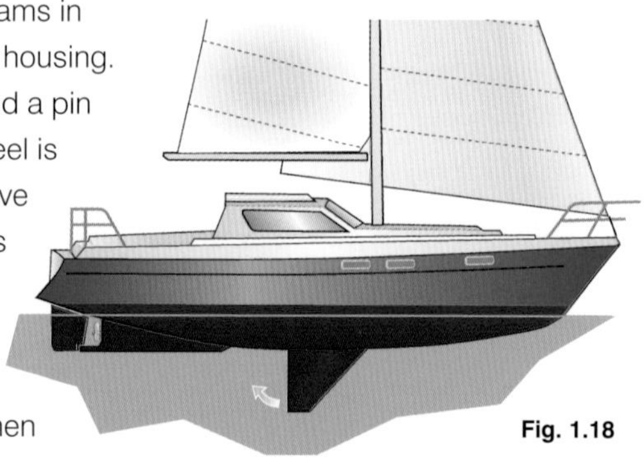

Fig. 1.18

Another much-heralded benefit is the ability to dry out upright, particularly when partnered with a twin rudder design. Nevertheless, some offshore sailors may feel that the added complexity and likelihood of failure outweighs all perceived advantages. Most sailors with lifting keel boats that I've spoken to have experienced, or continue to worry about, at least one of the following:

- That keel slot in the bottom of the boat. How well engineered is it to resist the side loads imposed on it by the centreplate?
- The rope and pulleys that operate the centreplate. When is something going to break?
- When are all the barnacles, firmly attached to the 'impossible to anti-foul' inner surfaces of the keel housing, going to gang-up and jam the centreplate?
- How soon before a stone wedges itself between the centreplate and the keel housing, firmly jamming it in the 'up' position?
- How much longer can I put up with the noise of the thing rattling around?

But they have their moments of glory. For a UK yachtsman tempted by the prospect of warm-water Mediterranean sailing, but not overly enthused about the exposed passage around the Iberian Peninsular and through the Straits of Gibraltar, a lifting keel boat will get him there through the Canal de Garonne and the Canal du Midi.

Twin, or Bilge Keels

These are a peculiarly British thing. Nowhere else do they seem to enjoy the same level of popularity. Along with long-legged birds and welly-clad bait diggers, they're very much at home on tidal mud flats, where drying moorings are much less expensive than the deep-water kind. Apart from their shallow draught, the benefit of a bilge keeler is that these cheap moorings can be enjoyed without falling over – twice a day in fact. And that's it, as far as I can see. Under way, their high wetted area and lack of low-down ballast can only detract from their sailing performance – and if you inadvertently run aground in one of these, you may be there for a while, since you can't heel the boat to reduce its draught.

Twin keeled craft usually have shallower draughts and the ability to take the ground upright

Fig. 1.19

Hull Material

Hulls should be both strong and rigid. A fairly obvious requirement you may think, but it isn't always the case, particularly with lightly built GRP hulls. Out of the water, a boat should be capable of taking all of its weight on its keel without undue hull distortion. Afloat, hardening-up both the forestay and backstay should create only minimum distortion. Metal hulls will flex the least and are strongest in terms of impact resistance.

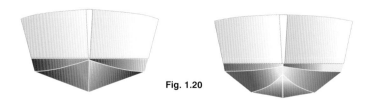

Fig. 1.20

GRP

Of the four basic materials – GRP, metal, wood and ferrocement – GRP (glass reinforced plastic) is the material of choice for production boats. Glassfibre, as it's universally known, is in its basic form polyester resin reinforced with chopped strand mat. Modern GRP designs employ more sophisticated laminates and often incorporate layers of stronger woven-glass rovings or exotic materials such as aramids (Kevlar®, Twaron®) to build in additional strength where it's needed. Fibreglass lends itself to mass-production techniques as, through investment in moulds and automated tooling, labour costs can be kept to a minimum and hulls of consistent quality produced in high volume. With its high strength-to-weight ratio, fibreglass is an ideal hull material provided that sufficient stiffening is built into the hull structure.

For low-volume production GRP is unsuitable owing to the high mould costs and the inability to amortise them over a large production run.

Steel

Steel is a favourite choice of material for the amateur or one-off builder, not just for the inherent strength of a metal hull, but also because of the relatively low cost of the raw material and the ease of construction for those with welding skills. Designs are either single chine, multi-chine or fully rounded. From an aesthetic point of view, the latter wins hands down. Steel suffers from chemical corrosion in saltwater, so it's absolutely vital to maintain a protective surface coat of a water-resistant paint – epoxy being the best choice. Because of its weight, steel is more suitable for hulls of 45ft and above.

Fig. 1.21

Aluminium

Aluminium is more difficult to weld than steel but has the advantage of a better strength-to-weight ratio, and it doesn't suffer from saltwater corrosion. In fact, some owners are happy to leave their vessels unfaired and unpainted, accepting with a Gallic shrug the appearance of the protective coating of aluminium oxide that quickly builds up. But aluminium is susceptible to electrolytic and galvanic corrosion by contact with dissimilar metals, or through improperly designed or installed electrical systems. Sacrificial zinc anodes are essential to keep galvanic corrosion at bay. Many owners, wary of stray electrical currents, choose to dangle a few additional ones over the side when in marina berths but a better form of protection would be to fit an 'isolating transformer' or a 'galvanic isolator' so there are no interactions with the marina's shore supply.

Wood

Modern wooden-hulled cruising boats will almost certainly be strip-planked and epoxy-sheathed. This technique lends itself to custom boat-building as no moulds are required, the hull being built upside down around temporary timber frames. The planks are glued one to the other with epoxy, and the completed hull is sheathed in layers of woven glass rovings and epoxy. Such hulls, more often than not of western red cedar, are light, strong and stiff, and require little maintenance. Being completely sealed, rot – the enemy of traditional wooden hulls – is not an issue.

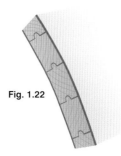

Fig. 1.22

Ferroconcrete

We're back in heavy-displacement territory here. Hull construction is an internal steel mesh structure plastered with a sand/cement mortar. Although the process is labour intensive, the construction materials are comparatively inexpensive, making them an attractive building option to someone with more time on his hands than cash in his pocket. Some ferroconcrete hulls will have been built by specialist boat-builders skilled in the technique, but the majority are home built. And herein lays the problem, as the quality of a ferroconcrete hull is totally dependent on the manner in which it has been built.

If the hull has been poorly constructed, for example with voids left in the mortar or with inadequate bonding to the mesh reinforcement, then it will be structurally unsound at best and may be very weak indeed.

Ferroconcrete boats are difficult to insure at reasonable premiums, some insurance companies being unwilling to provide cover at any price. As a result resale values are low.

2

SAILS & RIGS

For ultimate windward performance, nothing beats a deep-fin keeled monohull with a tall, high aspect ratio Bermudan rig. In plain English, low-aspect ratio sails are short and squat while high aspect ones are tall and narrow, or long and narrow like the wings on a high-performance glider.

Unlike gliders – which, being unrestrained by land or water, are always heading directly into the apparent wind – we aren't always beating to windward. In fact, most of us go to some lengths to avoid it if we can. Very high-aspect ratio rigs are only really appropriate for racing boats, where windward performance is vital for success. Such rigs rapidly lose their efficiency when even slightly off the wind, which is why offshore racing yachts carry extensive sail wardrobes. This is a route we cruising types don't want to go down, so extremes aren't for the likes of us.

But it remains true that, for windward performance, benefits are to be had by limiting the number of sails – a sloop will perform better than a ketch, for example. So why don't we all have sloops? Let's take a look at the various rigs and sail plans and discuss their pros and cons.

High aspect ratio

Fig. 2.1

Low aspect ratio

The Sloop Rig

Along with matchstick people and two-dimensional houses, the first sailboat a child draws is usually a sloop – a hull with a mast supporting two triangular sails. Not only are they easy to draw, they also offer simplicity and efficiency at the least practicable cost. And they come in two variants – masthead and fractional.

The masthead sloop is the simpler rig of the two, with the forestay attached at the top of the mast. Foresails of various sizes can be set on the forestay, from 'working' jibs through to large 130% deck-sweeping genoas. Foresails are called jibs if the clew doesn't reach farther aft than the mast, and genoas when it does. So the 'luff perpendicular', or LP (see fig. 2.2) of a 130% genoa is 30% longer than the distance between the mast and the stemhead – known as the 'J' measurement. Deck-sweeping genoas such as these create a wide blind-spot off the leeward bow. Unwanted surprises and chance encounters will be far fewer if the clew is cut higher, providing forward visibility from the cockpit under the foot of the sail.

With the fractional rig the forestay is attached at a point further down the mast, leaving the top section of the mast unsupported from forward. To maintain sail area the smaller jib is compensated by a larger main, which provides the following benefits:

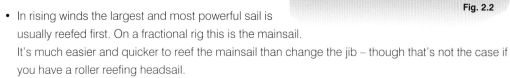

LP (Luff Perpendicular)

'J' (Base of the fore triangle)

Fig. 2.2

- In rising winds the largest and most powerful sail is usually reefed first. On a fractional rig this is the mainsail. It's much easier and quicker to reef the mainsail than change the jib – though that's not the case if you have a roller reefing headsail.
- With the shorter hoist spinnakers are smaller and easier to control than the larger ones flown on masthead sloops.
- Downwind, the larger main gives more drive, and it's not so important if the smaller jib is blanketed by it.
- By tensioning the backstay, the mast is deflected forward in the middle sections, flattening the mainsail, and thus maintaining drive while reducing heeling moment.

Of course there are downsides. The primary one is the requirement for running backstays to tension the forestay and keep the mast in column. These must be properly handled during tacking and gybing or you risk damaging, or even losing, the mast.

All offshore cruising sloops should have the capability of rigging a temporary inner forestay for hanking on a storm jib. Set on the 'outer' forestay a storm jib can cause lee helm, which is really what you don't want in heavy weather. The inner stay is stored against the mast when not in use, and deployed by attaching to a strongpoint on the foredeck using one of the several tensioning devices designed for this purpose.

The Cutter Rig

The flexibility and ease of handling of the cutter rig makes it the firm favourite of many offshore sailors, even though it's not quite as efficient to windward as a sloop. Essentially it's a masthead rig with two headsails and once again there are two variants – one where the jib is set on a bowsprit and the staysail attached to the bow; the other where the mast is positioned further aft and the whole rig contained inboard. The downside of a cutter is that you've got two headsails to deal with when going about, although a self-tacking boomed staysail eliminates this minor inconvenience.

Sloop or cutter, sail handling may all get a bit too much for a shorthanded crew on a boat any longer than 45 feet or so, without reliance upon power-driven sail-handling devices. At this point split rigs with their smaller individual sails begin to look attractive.

Exceptionally sturdy rigs make cutters a good choice for offshore cruising

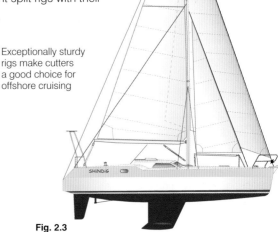

Fig. 2.3

Split Rigs: Ketches & Yawls

Ketches and yawls are two-masted rigs with a mainmast foremost and a smaller mizzen mast aft. It's generally accepted that the difference between the two types comes down to the location of the mast in relation to the rudder post. In a yawl the mizzen is aft of the rudder post and in the ketch it's forward. But the real difference is one of purpose. The mizzen on a yawl is intended to help trim the boat, in capable hands giving them the ability to follow a compass course despite minor wind shifts. These days, efficient autopilots and navigation aids have made this less important and the yawl has generally fallen out of favour. The mizzen sail of a ketch is larger than that of a yawl and is there to add drive. And so it does – off the wind. On the wind though, the mizzen is likely to add nothing but drag, being backwinded most of the time by the mainsail. In these conditions the mizzen may as well be dropped, at which point the ketch becomes in effect an undercanvassed sloop. Off the wind a ketch is at its most efficient, particularly so if cutter rigged and with a mizzen staysail set. But all the additional hardware – mizzen mast, sails, winches, standing and running rigging – comes with a considerable cost burden.

There are benefits to be had from a split rig. Firstly, they offer greater flexibility for sail reduction, allowing a jib and mizzen configuration in strong winds; and secondly, at anchor where, with the mizzen set as a steadying sail, the boat will lay comfortably head-to-wind.

Although you'll see many ketches with a triatic backstay between the two mastheads, each mast should be stayed individually. While this stay is ideally placed to act as an insulated SSB radio aerial, in the event of the loss of one mast it's almost guaranteed to result in the loss of the other. Lastly, the mizzen provides an ideal place to mount your radar scanner and wind generator.

Unstayed Rigs

Although often seen as a recent innovation, these have been with us for thousands of years – the Chinese junk being the best known example.

But in recent years the development of carbon fibre technology has enabled the concept to be brought up to date. Design and manufacturing techniques ensure adequate strength and stiffness is combined with light weight. All unstayed masts are keel-stepped as they rely entirely on the cantilever thus provided for support. The mast is subjected to bending moment only, with none of the compressive forces that a stayed mast has to withstand. The flexibility of the rig means that it's impossible to get sufficient forestay tension to support a conventional jib, so any such sail is likely to be a blade-type set-up on a fractionally rigged forestay. More often than not headsails are dispensed with altogether and a single-masted cat rig or ketch rig used – the Gary Hoyt-designed Freedom range being notable examples. Either conventional booms or wishbone rigs are used to support the clew of the sail. The wishbone rig greatly reduces the risk of head injury from an accidental gybe – a valuable safety feature indeed. Aerodynamically this rig is very clean – few yachtsmen will lament the loss of the rigging-induced whining when it starts to blow, but it does mean there's less to grab hold of when up on deck.

When seen alongside the complexity of a conventionally rigged vessel, it's easy to imagine that unstayed wishbone rigs may well represent the way ahead for offshore cruising designs.

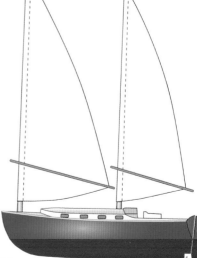

Unstayed rigs are aerodynamically clean but there's less to hold on to on deck

Fig. 2.4

Sails

It's wonderful stuff, wind. However much we sailors use, there's always lots left. Best of all, it's free.

Sails, sadly, aren't free. They must be carefully designed and accurately constructed from increasingly high-tech fabrics if they are to capture the energy of the wind and efficiently convert it to motive power.

For windward sailing, our sails must provide lift. This is generated through high-speed, low-pressure air on the convex side of the sail and low-speed, high-pressure air on the other. Drag, both aerodynamic and frictional, opposing forward momentum, is again an unwelcome but inevitable associate. An efficient windward sail must be cut to maximise lift and minimise drag.

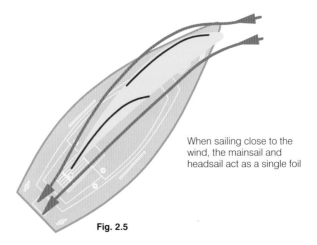

When sailing close to the wind, the mainsail and headsail act as a single foil

Fig. 2.5

RYA code G99

These days, sail design is carried out by professional designers using dedicated software to produce both the overall three-dimensional curvature, and the shape of the individual flat panels that go to make up the whole. It remains for the sailmaker to use his skill and expertise to sew them together into a robust sail that takes up the desired shape when filled with wind. For more guidance, see G99 RYA Sail Trim Handbook for Cruisers.

Sail Cloth

The sailmaker has two fundamentally different types of fabric to choose from:

- Woven fabric, in which the material is produced by weaving fibres one over the other in a loom
- Laminates, which are made by gluing together alternate layers of plastic film and reinforcing grids of synthetic fibres

Woven Fabrics

Apart from its shape, two primary factors influence the performance of a woven sail, the modulus of the fibres, and the closeness of the weave.

The modulus, derived from Young's Modulus of Elasticity, is a measure of the fibre's resistance to stretch – high modulus being less stretchy.

For we cruising sailors the desire for pure sail performance will be tempered by the sail's initial cost and longevity in use. Not for us are the high-end, very low stretch and very expensive aramid fibres (such as Kevlar® and Twaron®, for example) which are often inferior to polyester fibres when it comes to ultra-violet (UV) degradation, fatigue and abrasion resistance.

Polyester fibre, often known by its trade name Dacron®, is the most common fibre used for woven sailcloth. Its properties include good UV, fatigue and abrasion resistance, and it's comparatively inexpensive. Other woven fabrics used in cruising sails include the following High Modulus Poly-Ethylene (HMPE) fibres, which are similarly identified by their trade names Spectra® and Dyneema®. They're all more expensive than polyester fibres:

- HMPE fibres are lightweight but durable, having excellent fatigue, UV and abrasion resistance. This type has a higher modulus than polyester and is often specified for performance cruising sails.
- Vectran® has a modulus five times greater than polyester, and is reputed to have less stretch and to be more durable than HMPE, but is more expensive and less UV resistant unless properly protected.
- PEN (Polyethylene naphthalate) fibres, commonly known by the trade name Pentex®, have twice the modulus of polyester and slightly better UV resistance.
- Nylon is traditionally used for spinnakers owing to its very light weight, but its stretch resistance isn't great.

The Warp and the Weft

As with all woven fabrics, sailcloth is made up of yarns perpendicular to each other. Those running across the loom are the 'weft' – or 'fill' in the United States – and those longitudinal to it the 'warp'. Most woven fabrics are weft orientated as it's easier to control the tension in this short direction across the width of the loom.

Consequently, woven sailcloth generally – but not always – has greater stretch resistance across the width of the roll, and less along its length. When stressed diagonally across both warp and weft – on the 'bias' as it's known – woven fabrics have least resistance and deform easily. Sailmakers therefore contrive to arrange the fabric panels such that the warp or weft (depending on the orientation) aligns with the tensile force in the sail. Fig. 2.7 indicates approximately where these are to be found in headsails and mainsails. In the headsail, tension is applied to the luff by the halyard and in approximately equal amounts to the foot and the leech by the sheet. The most highly tensioned part of the mainsail is the luff, applied by the mainsheet and at its maximum when hard on the wind.

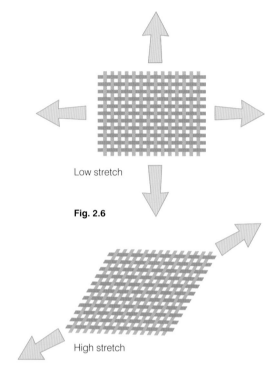

Low stretch

Fig. 2.6

High stretch

Cross-cut and Radial Sails

Until computers enabled us properly to understand the stress patterns in sails and the distortion characteristics of the fabrics, sails were fabricated in cross-cut fashion using weft-orientated fabric. Although radially cut sails are known to hold their shape better than cross-cuts, smaller sails, where the gain would be minimal, are still usually cross-cut. As size increases, the improved directional stability of a radial sail becomes increasingly desirable.

There's considerably more fabric wastage in the fabrication of a radially cut sail and a lot more stitching involved. It'll come as no surprise that they're more expensive than cross-cuts.

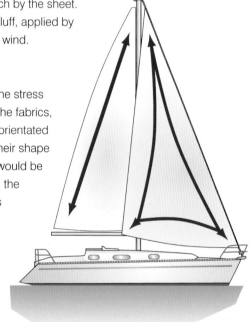

Fig. 2.7 The red arrows show the general orientation of loads in the sails

Laminates

This sail fabric is built up of layers of film, scrim and taffeta glued together under high temperature and pressure to form a light, strong composite sail fabric.

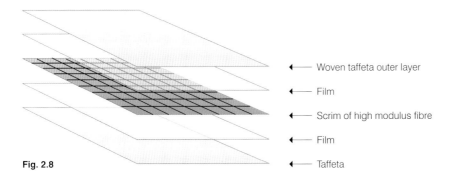

Woven taffeta outer layer

Film

Scrim of high modulus fibre

Film

Fig. 2.8   Taffeta

The film is a sheet of isotropic plastic, most often a Mylar® extrusion, which has very low stretch characteristics in all directions, including the bias.

The scrim is a grid of large, unwoven, straight fibres which may be polyester, one of the HMPE varieties, or even more exotic fibres such as carbon. Scrims have very little stretch in the direction of the fibres, and are often bonded with other scrims of different orientation.

Taffeta is a woven fabric, most often polyester, that makes up the outside surfaces of the laminate, and is there to provide durability, and UV and chafe resistance to the sail. Laminate sails are lighter than woven sails and have a higher modulus. As most of the scrim is usually orientated on the warp, the panels can be cut in long, narrow triangular shapes ideally suited to accommodate the stress patterns in a radially cut sail. Although having become cheaper in recent years, the cost of a laminate sail remains higher than that of a woven sail of similar strength and size. Nevertheless, their improved robustness and durability means that they are seen with increasing frequency on offshore cruising boats.

Moulded Sails

Sails built up in a series of bonded-together flat panels can only ever approximate – albeit very closely – to the computerised perfection created by the designer.

A moulded sail is a laminate built up on a computer-designed female mould, and only then glued together under pressure with the designed double curvature accurately built in.

Moulded sails are made in reasonably large numbers for one-design racing boats, which enables the mould and tooling costs to be amortised. They can also be seen on large one-off sponsored racing boats, where they have completed round-the-world events without a problem, removing any doubts as to their durability. Manufacturers are striving to make inroads into the cruising market, but for the moment at least they remain prohibitively expensive for most of us.

Reefing & Furling Systems

I suppose some gung-ho types revel in changing foresails in the dark on a pitching foredeck in a rising gale. I don't and never did – come to think of it, I don't know anyone who does. So to all manufacturers of headsail furling gears – thank you. It's undeniably true that a partially furled genoa will never be quite as efficient as a hanked-on jib of the same size, but for the cruising sailor the small performance loss is balanced by the rapid adjustment of headsail power they deliver.

Some systems improve efficiency by using a double-swivel arrangement which puts a full roll into the middle of the sail before the rotation is taken up by the head and the tack. This goes some way towards removing the fullness that would otherwise be present in the partially rolled sail. Sailmakers have done their bit too by building a foam insert into the luff, which similarly flattens a partially rolled headsail.

Modern systems are very reliable and require little maintenance. The most common problem is not one of equipment failure, but one of incorrect set-up. If the luff of the sail is much shorter than the foil, the halyard can – and according to Murphy, undoubtedly will – get twisted around the foil, comprehensively jamming up the works. Prevention is quite simple – a short wire strop between the top swivel and the head of the sail.

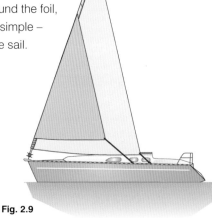

Fig. 2.9

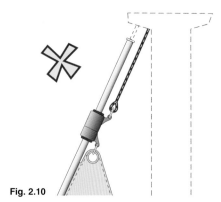

Fig. 2.10

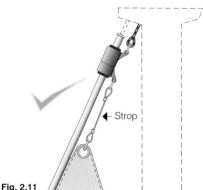

← Strop

Fig. 2.11

As mentioned earlier, deck-sweeping genoas are not wonderful if you're at all interested in what's going on ahead; nor do they work well with furling gear unless you're happy to move the sheet traveller every time you adjust the furler. It's a geometry thing, and as shown in fig. 2.11 a higher clew will enable the headsail to be rolled progressively without having to adjust the position of the car. Whether you sail in Arctic waters, the tropics, or anywhere in between, a sacrificial strip is essential to protect the sail from UV damage when fully furled.

The roller reefing technology has crept into mainsail systems, and much less successfully in my view. There are two approaches to this – in-mast systems and in-boom systems.

I reckon there's nothing wrong with the simplicity of slab reefing and lazy-jacks. Even on boats of 45 feet and above, the difficulty of hoisting a heavy fully battened mainsail can be overcome by an electric winch and, with all lines led aft, slab reefing can still be feasible. A pal of mine sails his Sundeer 64 single-handed without undue drama using this approach, and wouldn't have it any other way. When I see Mike Golding and his mates racing alone around the world in their hugely powerful machines using anything other than this system for mainsail handling, then maybe I'll think again.

In-mast Systems

At best, this is a quick and easy way – providing you get the procedure right – to reduce the area of the mainsail in a rising wind. But it can go wrong – and if it does with the sail jammed in the mast groove you won't be able to get it in, out, up, down or do anything much at all with it, unless you have a bosun's chair and a sharp knife. Sails used with this system are flat cut, have little or no roach – or even a negative roach – and if there are any battens at all, they'll be vertical – and there's a penalty to be paid in additional weight aloft as a result of the all the hardware inside the mast.

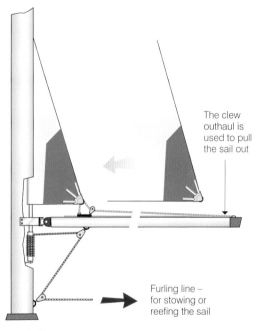

The clew outhaul is used to pull the sail out

Furling line – for stowing or reefing the sail

Fig. 2.12

In-boom Systems

In-boom systems use a fully battened mainsail and are conceptually more seaworthy than the in-mast type, because:

- If the sail jams in the boom slot, it's still possible to ease the halyard and drop it.
- A sail jammed in the boom slot will be much easier to sort out than one halfway up the mast.
- Reefing the sail in the boom lowers the centre of gravity, unlike the in-mast system which leaves the weight of the sail aloft.

For successful operation the angle between the boom and the mast is critical. In some systems this is fixed by a rigid kicker, while others allow a degree of articulation and rely on a spring in the kicker to return the boom to its correct angle. The double swivel arrangement found on headsail furlers is also incorporated in some in-boom systems, which flatten the main without reducing its area.

Slab Reefing

If you haven't guessed it already, I unashamedly admit that this is the one for me. Simple, efficient and reliable, it is the essence of a seaworthy system. With all control lines at the mast – main halyard, topping lift and reefing lines – one person can pull a reef in on his own. Alternatively all lines can be led aft, and all reefing done from the security of the cockpit.

A common, but in my view daft, arrangement is where the reefing lines are led back to the cockpit, but the halyard and the reef cringles have to be dealt with at the mast – the worst of both worlds.

If the cockpit arrangement is your preference then the single-line reefing system available from some spar makers is worth considering. These only accommodate the first two reefs, which is fine most of the time but when you really need the third reef a trip to the mast is unavoidable just when it appeals least. A better arrangement with this system is to have just two deep reefs in the main and to hoist the trysail when the going gets really tough.

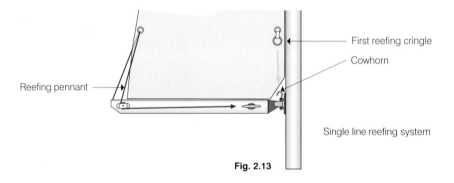

First reefing cringle

Cowhorn

Reefing pennant

Single line reefing system

Fig. 2.13

Flying cringle

For the mast-based alternative, a couple of innovations make the task of dealing with the luff cringle much easier – captive hooks and 'flying' cringles as shown in the photograph to the right.

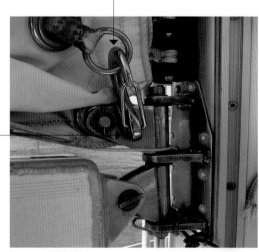

Captive hook better than cringle

Improved luff cringle arrangement better than cowhorn

Reefing Lines

The correct way to secure the reefing lines around the boom is shown in fig. 2.14. With a loose-footed main the tendency is for this locking loop to migrate towards the mast, allowing a reef to be pulled down without applying any tension to the foot and resulting in a baggy reefed sail. Such a sail shape will produce more heeling moment than drive, but tying the loops back to the end of the boom prevents this happening.

Fig. 2.14

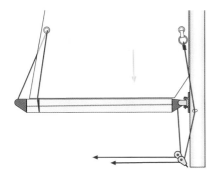

Fig. 2.15 Two line reefing system

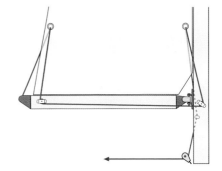

Fig. 2.16 Jiffy reefing system

Lazyjacks

While these efficiently collect the main and guide it onto the boom as it's dropped, they are equally efficient at trapping the ends of the battens as the sail is raised. The solution is simple – slacken them off, pull them forward and secure them on the mast. The reefing hooks, if you have them, are ideally placed for this.

A very nifty sail cover can be combined with lazyjacks. With one of these 'stack-packs' the sail can be dropped and the cover zipped in half the time it takes to drag a conventional mainsail cover out of its locker. A convincing argument and a convenient solution, but they spoil the airflow around the foot of the sail and, along with the coloured sacrificial strips on furling headsails, look awful under sail.

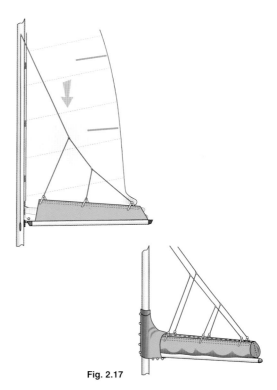

Fig. 2.17

Fully Battened Mainsails

These first became popular on racing multihulls, primarily to support the large roach that the absence of a central backstay allowed them to carry. Other benefits of more interest to cruisers are:

- In light winds this sail still provides drive in conditions where a short-battened main would tend to collapse, and,
- when coming up to wind to reduce sail, this sail is less likely to flog, sparing the nerves of the crew and extending the life of the sail.

On the downside, there's obviously more weight aloft and an increased risk of chafe where the battens rub against the rigging when sailing off the wind.

To take up the desired shape, the battens are forced into compression by adjustment at the leech-end pocket. Without substantial sockets and specially designed slides, the resultant pressure on the mast would make it impossible to hoist or lower these sails. Some very slick systems are available, involving an external mast track and ball-bearing cars.

You may think that a much less sophisticated halfway-house system would be more suitable for an offshore cruising yacht. Here, only the top two battens are full length, preserving the sail shape where it's most needed. These relatively short full battens won't need the same degree of compression to assume the required curve. Cheap and easily replaced low-friction slides, designed for a standard mast groove, can now be used.

Or No Battens at All?

Having put a few sea miles into your smart new mainsail, it's odds on that the first area requiring maintenance will be the batten pockets.

For some skippers who are prepared to accept a reduced sail area, this vulnerability is a compelling reason for managing without them. Battens exist to support the luff, but if the luff is slightly hollow it will support itself and battens become redundant.

A variation on this theme, as used by a pal of mine, is to have the sail cut with a conservative roach at the head of the sail supported by two full battens and a hollow luff below with no battens. It works for him.

Loose Footed Mains

A necessity with in-mast reefing systems and an impossibility with in-boom systems, there's much to be said for loose-footed mains in conjunction with slab reefing and lazyjacks.

- Firstly, the sail shape extends to the foot, unlike those which are restrained in the groove in the boom.
- Secondly, the absence of friction allows the foot tension to be adjusted quickly and easily.

The Boom

The function of the boom is to maintain the position of the mainsail clew at any point of sail. Foot tension is provided by the outhaul and leech tension by the mainsheet when on the wind, and the vang (or kicker) when off it. In light airs the topping lift is used to prevent the weight of the boom from dragging the shape out of the sail. The outhaul normally takes the form of a track-mounted car, but on booms intended for use with

This arrangement shows an outhaul lever rather than the more usual outhaul car

loose-footed mains it's often replaced by a simple lever. The outhaul control line can be brought back to the cockpit, but it's more often adjusted via a jamming cleat mounted on the side of the boom.

The mechanical advantage of the mainsheet depends on the number of parts in its tackle and the location of the point at which it's attached to the boom. Various mainsheet options are available, including a two-speed system combining a 4:1 coarse (fast) adjustment and a 8:1 fine (slow) adjustment. Unavoidably, increasing the mechanical advantage involves a proportional increase in the amount of rope, and more blocks.

Similarly, the efficiency of the kicker depends not only on the number of parts in its tackle but also on its angle in relation to the boom. The flatter the angle, the greater the compressive component of force that's applied to the boom and the lesser the downforce – which is not what you want. There are rope kickers and there are rigid kickers. The pros and cons are:

Rope Kickers:

Pros – simple, little to go wrong and if it breaks you can fix it

Cons – will only pull the boom down, so you'll need a topping lift to hold it up

Rigid Kickers:

Pros – eliminates the need for a topping lift

Cons – more difficult to repair, may need replacement in event of failure

– prevents dropping of boom on deck, which you may need to do to fly a trysail

– expensive

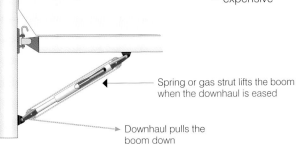

Spring or gas strut lifts the boom when the downhaul is eased

Downhaul pulls the boom down

Fig. 2.18 Typical rigid kicker

The topping lift can be set up in one of two ways:

- Much like a second main halyard, attached to the end of the boom, or,
- as a line fixed at the masthead and attached to the end of the boom via a short two-part tackle.

The latter option is more efficient as it requires less rope and avoids the severe change of direction at the masthead. However, provided the topping lift is of appropriate strength, the first option enables it to be used as a halyard for the trysail.

The Mast

Keel or deck-stepped, in engineering terms the mast is a column with compressive loads applied by the standing rigging. Leonhard Paul Euler (1707–1783), a Swiss mathematician and physicist, probably didn't know one end of a yacht from the other but did provide us with the theory that structural engineers and mast designers rely on. Euler established that a column will buckle long before the applied load would cause it to fail in pure compression, and went on to prove that the load at which buckling failure will occur depends on the 'slenderness ratio'. This is expressed as the effective length of the column divided by the radius of gyration of the column section – the l/r ratio.

In their quest for reduced windage and mainsail shape control, designers of racing and some racer/cruiser rigs push the slenderness ratio to the limit, relying on elaborate lateral support provided by multiple pairs of spreaders and complicated sets of shrouds. These finely tuned, unforgiving structures require a high degree of operator expertise and maintenance. They have no place on an offshore cruising yacht. For cruising sailors, mast failure is a catastrophe that should be avoided at all costs.

Cost may well be the operative word, as mast failure on a cruising rig is much more likely to arise from the failure of the fittings on the mast, rather than the section itself.

Through-bolted tangs and eyes are the most secure method of attaching shrouds to the mast and T-bars and stem ball(s) probably the least.

Often seen in masthead assemblies, goosenecks, spreader sockets and kicker attachments, alloy castings are always suspect. There may be voids or other defects within which are totally invisible from the outside. For these fittings, welded fabrications are more reliable than castings.

It's vital that standing rigging is free to articulate at each end to accommodate the natural flexing that will occur. Otherwise, if misaligned or restricted in movement at all, stainless steel rigging will quickly fatigue and fail. For this reason the lower ends of all shrouds and stays must be fitted with toggles. Aloft, toggles are only required on the forestay (and cutter stay, if fitted) to take up the lateral movement caused by the headsail and staysail.

On multi-spreader rigs, discontinuous rigging terminates at the spreader ends rather than on deck. As a result it uses less material and therefore reduces weight aloft. The better articulation also reduces metal fatigue and simplifies the job of tuning the rig.

Fractional rigs and cutter rigs are normally associated with running backstays, a contrivance viewed with some disdain by many cruising sailors. There are other ways of supporting these rigs –

aft-swept spreaders and aft intermediate shrouds – but both give rise to other problems that you may feel outweigh any benefit:

- Aft-swept spreaders limit the amount by which you can square off the main without chafing the sail on the spreader ends. Tuning the rig is also much more difficult.
- Aft intermediates are only a few degrees off vertical, so to get any meaningful aft component of force they must be highly tensioned. This puts a lot of compression on the mast and additional load on the chain plates.

Rigging screws – or turnbuckles as our American friends call them – are used to tension the standing rigging, although hydraulic rams may be used on the backstays of larger vessels. Very often the central body part and the stud ends are machined from stainless steel, which is not quite as sensible as it may first seem.

Turning these under high loads can cause the threads to gall and seize together, but this risk can be avoided by using either all-bronze components, or a bronze body and stainless studs.

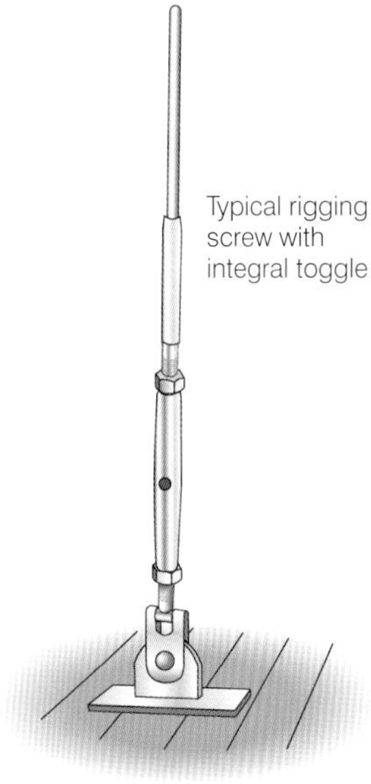

Some years ago I was sailing my Nicholson 32 single-handed from Moraira on the Spanish Costa Blanca to Ibiza. Conditions were perfect, the sun was shining, not a cloud in the sky and *Jalingo II* was bowling along nicely. I was idly watching my mate 'Arry' doing his thing, 'Arry' being the Aries self-steering gear. A periodic glance ahead and something shiny on the foredeck caught my eye. What was it? A clevis pin! A most urgent inspection took place. The rig was still there, which was a good sign. The windward shrouds were taut and there was nothing flapping on the leeward side. A close inspection at deck level revealed that everything was as it should be and the binoculars confirmed a similar situation aloft. Much relieved, I could only assume that a higher authority had decided I was having far too much fun. Or maybe it had fallen from my spares kit. Either way, it reminded me just how much the rig depends on these small items. Love your clevis pins and protect them. They are designed for shear loads, not bending, so toggles must fit snugly around them. Left to their own devices, they will wriggle out, with calamitous results, so they must be securely retained. Split pins – cotter pins in the USA – are good provided they're installed correctly. Split rings are a poor substitute. If subjected to chafe – a flogging sheet for example – they'll deform, rotate and can fall out – whereupon down will come baby, cradle and all.

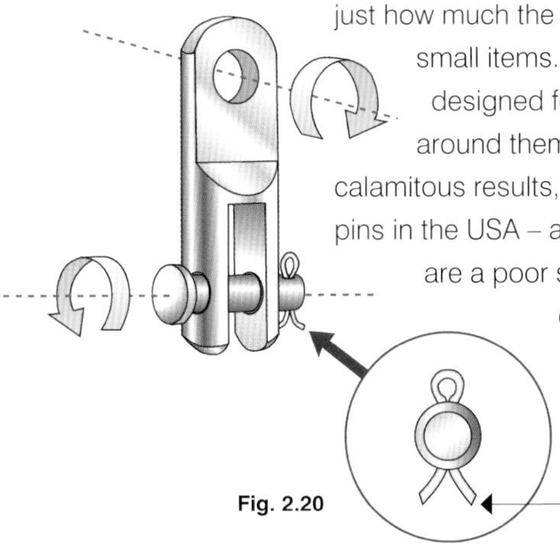

Typical rigging screw with integral toggle

Fig. 2.19

Fig. 2.20

Split pin should be opened up no more than a few degrees

Keel-stepped or Deck-stepped?

Conventional wisdom has it that for offshore sailing boats, the masts should be keel-stepped because:

- If a shroud parts the mast is likely to remain standing, supported by the cantilever provided by the keel step and the partners.
- In the event of a capsize any damage to the mast is most likely to occur some distance above the deck, leaving a mast stub available for a jury rig.

But unless the deck is massively strong at the partners this area is likely to suffer structural damage, which in conditions severe enough to cause a capsize will be very serious indeed. A lesser problem is that rainwater always gets inside the mast through the various openings and a keel-stepped mast ensures that this ends up in the bilge rather than draining out on deck.

A mast stepped on deck must be supported by a compression post below, which will transfer all mast loads to the keel. Structurally, the mast is pinjointed in the deck-mounted baseplate. This facilitates easier removal at layup time, but does make it more likely that if you lose your mast, you're going to lose all of it.

Light Weather and Downwind

In a following breeze, the large stable area of a 'wing and wing' set-up provides reasonable performance, but with the jib poled out and the main secured against an accidental gybe by a preventer, you'd be ill-advised to be crossing shipping lanes with this sail configuration. Sloops perform well set-up thus, but cutters much less so, penalised as they are by the relatively small area of the yankee and the now redundant staysail.

In light winds, and particularly if sailing downwind, many sailors furl the headsail and reach for the ignition keys. Others may still furl the headsail, but hoist one of the following in its place.

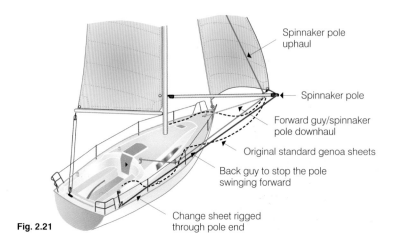

Spinnaker pole uphaul

Spinnaker pole

Forward guy/spinnaker pole downhaul

Original standard genoa sheets

Back guy to stop the pole swinging forward

Change sheet rigged through pole end

Fig. 2.21

Lightweight Genoa

Sometimes called multi-purpose genoas, these are designed for windward sailing in light conditions when the working headsail is too small or heavy to produce much drive. They are set flying, so there's no need to remove the furled headsail, and, as long as they're set inside it, can be tacked in the normal way.

These radially cut nylon sails are intended for apparent wind speeds up to 12 knots and perform well in the range between close-hauled and a beam reach. Often incorporating an HMPE luff to enable it to be properly tensioned, they can be used with a lightweight furler.

Gennaker

This is what you need when the wind moves further aft and the lightweight genoa collapses. Gennaker, cruising chute, asymmetric or multi-purpose spinnakers are essentially all the same thing, although I've heard the asymmetric described as 'a cruising chute on steroids'.

Hoisted on the spinnaker halyard and controlled by a sheet led through a block on the quarter, spinnaker-like performance can be had on all points of sail from a close reach to a broad reach without any of the trauma. When close-reaching, the adjustable tack line is pulled down, tightening the luff and encouraging the sail to act more like a genoa. They're at the operating limit when the wind is on the quarter – any further aft and they'll be blanketed by the main and will collapse.

It's very likely that the foredeck layout, and particularly the pulpit, won't have been designed with one of these sails in mind. There'll probably be nowhere ahead of the forestay you can attach a tackline block to – and if there is, the tackline will chafe against the pulpit or the bow anchor.

Fig. 2.22

Short removable bowsprit

All of these problems would be solved by a short bowsprit. At least one spar manufacturer has recognised this and has produced a very neat device that's attached to a ring on the foredeck and is restrained by a collar fixed to the stemhead fitting. As it's removable you won't get charged for it in marinas. Set further forward the sail will be operating in clearer air, and will be more efficient as a result.

There are three designs for asymmetrics. All are radially cut, and each has a slightly different application:

- Starcut: a slightly flatter cut than the next two, and optimised for reaching.
- Radial head: cut fuller than the starcut, and with wider shoulders. More stable downwind than the starcut, but less so closer to the wind.
- Tri-radial: probably the best all-rounder for most of us, easily trimmed and with an operating range of 70° to 160° of the wind.

Starcut   Radial Head   Tri-radial

Fig. 2.23

If you're set on sailing dead downwind in light conditions and have a telescopic whisker pole to hand, there's no reason why you shouldn't pole out the clew and sail wing and wing. Alternatively, you could rig it as a conventional spinnaker as described below.

Spinnakers

Unlike their asymmetric brothers, which are tacked to the centreline, the tack of a conventional spinnaker is attached to the end of a pole which can be squared-off to the wind. Now operating in clear air, unaffected by the mainsail, this sail will propel you dead downwind. This performance benefit comes at the cost of complexity. Positioning the end of the pole at the correct position in space requires three control lines – a guy, a pole uphaul and a downhaul. The clew is controlled by a sheet led through a block on the quarter. In gusty conditions – where this sail's reputation for being unmanageable is usually gained – rapid adjustment to sheet and guy is required.

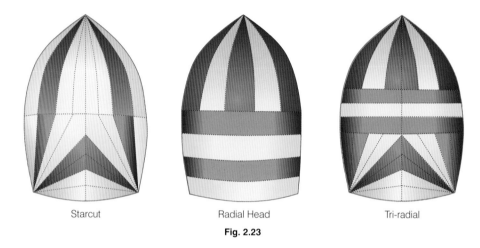

Spinnaker pole uphaul

Spinnaker

Note the guy runs through the pole end

Spinnaker pole downhaul

Working guy

Lazy sheet

Lazy guy

Working sheet

Fig. 2.24 Spinnaker hoisted with gear

If allowed to get out of control, heavy rolling can develop, leading in all probability to a broach. A broach to leeward is no fun, but a windward broach (putting the spinnaker pole into the water and causing a crash gybe of the boom and mainsail) can have very serious consequences indeed.

Many cruising sailors view all of this with a deal of trepidation, but others – often those used to inshore racing around the cans – gleefully drag out the spinnaker bag whenever the wind gets aft of the beam.

Snuffers

While racing crews will launch their spinnakers ('throw the kite up', as they may nonchalantly remark) directly from the spinnaker bag and subsequently wrestle it to the deck at the leeward mark, we cruisers should give a collective vote of thanks for the existence of the snuffer.

These devices, aka socks or squeezers, allow us both to launch and douse our spinnakers and gennakers with dignity and control. Preparation and awareness though, as with most endeavours, is everything. On launching, the goal should be for an immediate stable set, which is best achieved by pre-marking the control lines and adjusting them accordingly before operating the snuffer. The mistake of not having fully hoisted the sail, or of not having properly secured the halyard, is one that will remain in your memory for a while.

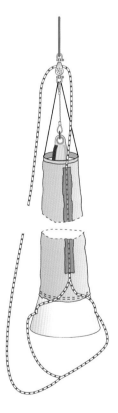

Hoisting
Hoist the sail to its full height in its sock.
Secure the tack line, then ease the sock line and trim on the sheet.
The sock will lift to the head as the sail fills

Dropping
Ease the sheet and haul on the sock line.
Once the sail is secure in its sock it can be lowered to the deck.

Fig. 2.25 Using a spinnaker sock

Tradewind Sailing

The stuff of dreams. Blue skies, fluffy white clouds, a deep blue sea and long gentle ocean swells. The warm breeze over the transom keeps the boat bowling along nicely and the miles reel off towards your exotic, tropical destination. Well, it can be like that, but conditions are often considerably more boisterous and the boat will be rolling, probably rather a lot.

With a roll period of, say, six seconds, she'll roll 10 times a minute, or 600 times an hour, or 14,400 times a day, or around 300,000 times on the tradewind passage from the Canary Islands to the West Indies. Line squalls will bowl in from astern, often accompanied by heavy rain and strong winds. With a poled-out jib and a main secured by a preventer, rounding up into the wind to put a reef in will be no fun at all. Life will be more agreeable all round with no main and twin headsails, and a twin-luff headsail gear lends itself very nicely to this rig.

Twin Headsails

Rather than hoisting two headsails at the same time, each in their respective luff groove, a better approach is to attach a good-quality block to the head shackle on the top swivel and reeve a 6mm Spectra® halyard through it with both ends tied off to the tack swivel on the furling drum. The usual headsail can be hoisted and operated in the normal way and the second headsail hoisted only when needed.

Fig. 2.26

When hoisting the second headsail, make sure that the luff groove is facing forward – if it isn't, a gybe will ensure that it is. If you try to hoist the sail with the groove facing aft, the wind will blow the sail around the foil and the resulting friction will be such that you won't be able to hoist the sail. With two headsails set in this way, they can be furled simultaneously if a squall comes through.

In the absence of a spare luff groove, the second headsail can be set flying, but this is likely to induce more rolling than the twin-luff set-up. Either way, the twin headsails will be more stable if they are of similar size and supported by similar length poles.

Without a second pole, the boom can be squared off and the jib sheet passed through a block on its end. This, though, is a poor substitute.

The Twistleyard Rig

With this development of the twin-pole system, the poles aren't attached to the mast – they butt into an articulated coupling that's supported above the foredeck by an uphaul and a downhaul. By adjusting the sheets, the twins can accommodate changes in the wind direction while maintaining their shape and projected area. This arrangement is reputed to reduce rolling greatly, as the poles are free

to float around rather than transferring lateral moment-inducing loads to the mast. Skippers of cutters may be disappointed to find that all the floating around needs to take place exactly where the cutter stay is.

Storm Canvas

If you sail long enough and far enough the odds are that sooner or later you'll be caught in conditions where you'd be better off with dedicated storm sails aloft. The primary requirements of these sails are that they:

- Must be very robustly constructed of heavyweight sail cloth
- Must be of a size suitable for the boat
- Should be highly visible against a grey and white sea

Every offshore cruising boat should carry a storm jib and trysail. Hove-to under these sails, a well-found yacht should be capable of riding out all but nature's most testing conditions. Long-keelers will heave-to like somnolent ducks, but fin and skeg sloops may find the required sail balance difficult to achieve with the storm jib set on the forestay, or on a removable inner forestay set immediately aft of it. Ideally, an inner forestay rigged about ⅓ of the J measurement aft of the forestay should be available for a storm jib. A spare jib halyard must be used – not the spinnaker halyard, which will chafe on the forestay, where its ultimate failure will be but a matter of time.

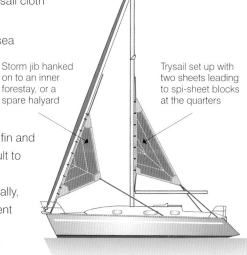

Storm jib hanked on to an inner forestay, or a spare halyard

Trysail set up with two sheets leading to spi-sheet blocks at the quarters

Fig. 2.27 Storm sails

Owners of cutters who've resisted the temptation to install their staysail on a furling gear have reason to feel pretty smug at this point, as their storm jib can now be simply hanked-on in place of their staysail.

A separate mast track should be provided for the trysail, which should be sheeted through a block on the quarter rather than to the end of the boom. Ideally the boom should be dropped on deck and secured, lowering the centre of gravity, reducing windage and negating its skull-crunching malevolence, but this won't be an option if you've a rigid kicker.

Well before the onset of heavy weather, the sail slides should be fed into the track, a pin inserted beneath to stop it falling out, and the bagged sail secured at the foot of the mast, ready for deployment. A prudent skipper will make sure that there's an end-stop at the top of the track to save embarrassment in the event of not having properly secured the tack before hoisting.

With a careful eye on the weather forecast and due regard to the recommended sailing seasons in various parts of the world,

Bagged storm trisail ready to hoist at foot of mast

your storm sails should see little use. But this can be no excuse for not having things all worked out beforehand, for when you do need them in earnest it's a little late to be wondering which end goes up and which corner should have sheet on it.

3

ON DECK

At sea the deck is a working platform, from which we need to operate with a reasonable chance of staying on it. Going forward in lively conditions, a succession of secure handholds – grabrails, guardwires and standing rigging – should present themselves within grabbing range and any surfaces we may need to stand on must be non-slip. Rounded edges to coamings and cabin tops – an example of form following fashion rather than function – are particularly treacherous when wet, as are deck hatches. The moulded texture found on GRP decks is seldom satisfactory, and in many cases has the non-skid characteristics of greased PTFE. Teak decks are very fashionable but, contrary to popular opinion, don't offer wonderful security underfoot when wet. Non-skid paint, which gets its non-skiddiness through particles suspended in it, works acceptably well wet or dry – without, in more clement conditions, causing howls of protest from owners of bikini-clad bottoms. Probably the best non-slip performance is offered by cork compound stick-on panels such as those manufactured under the Treadmaster trademark by Tiflex Ltd, but which will leave a lasting impression on the aforementioned owners. But if we are still unlucky enough to trip or stumble we should be prevented from the ultimate disaster by our safety harness and the guardwires.

Harnesses, Safety Lines and Jackstays

The primary function of a harness isn't to keep you attached to the boat after you've fallen over the side – it's to prevent you from going over in the first place. A fundamental requirement is that they're easy to put on. Some models though, apparently designed by the same person who creates those infuriating metal puzzles found inside Christmas crackers, require more mental and physical gymnastics than would seem reasonable.

Importantly, the clips used on the tethers should be of the safety type (see fig. 3.1) and not traditional caribiners which can accidentally unclip in some circumstances.

'Ocean'-type foul weather jackets remove this source of vexation by having them built in, but you'd find these very cumbersome in the tropics, where a lighter inshore version will be much more comfortable.

I've two harnesses, one incorporating a self-inflating life jacket adjusted to fit over a jacket, and the other standard type adjusted for the more lightly adorned McClary torso. On deck at night, in even benign conditions, you should always wear a harness.

A highly recommended arrangement is to position pad eyes in the cockpit so that lifelines can be hooked on, brought forward and dangled through the main hatch. This will enable you to hook-up below and remain secure while in transit between cabin and cockpit.

Jackstays, one either side, should run the full length of the deck from cockpit to bow. If fitted inboard along the coach roof rather than along the outer edge of the side-decks they've a greater chance of saving you from getting very wet. It's good practice to leave a lifeline hooked on to the after end of each jackstay and brought back to the cockpit. Now you can hook-up in readiness to go forward without first disconnecting from the cockpit pad-eye. The carbine hooks at each end of the lifeline should be fitted with spring-loaded struts that prevent their accidental release.

Fig. 3.1

Non-rattling lifeline pad-eye in cockpit

Webbing jackstay attached to foredeck pad-eye

Plastic-coated wire jackstays have an unfortunate tendency to roll underfoot, in doing so promoting the very event that they're supposed to protect against. I much prefer heavy-duty webbing straps which lie flat against the deck. With stainless 'D' rings sewn into each end these are lashed to fold-flat pad-eyes and are easily removed when not at sea to delay the onset of UV degradation.

Guardwires, Pulpits and Sternrails

These should create a continuous enclosure around the boat to a height of at least 600mm – 700mm is better. As the last line of defence against a possibly tragic event they must be structurally dependable. Stanchion bases, which will take a high rotational load if a crew member falls against the guardwire, must be properly secured to the side-deck by at least three bolts and a substantial backing plate. The guardwires must be checked regularly for damage and corrosion, and their anchorage points on pulpits and sternrails must be robust and corrosion-free as these too will take a high load in a fall. The top guardwire should be white plastic covered for visibility in poor light, and should have a swaged eye at the cockpit end, and/or a Norseman® or Staylock® fitting at the forward end to enable its removal.

The cringle should be lashed to the pushpit by half-a-dozen turns of 2mm Dyneema® shock-cord, which will be stronger than 5mm stainless steel wire, and will provide several benefits:

- It will be easy to tension, and
- it will be easy to cut in an emergency

Of passing interest to those who choose to do their reefing from the cockpit, granny bars – a politically incorrect term if ever I heard one – provide additional security when working at the mast, and useful handholds when going forward.

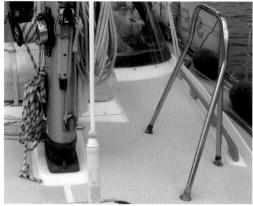
Sturdy granny bars make working at the mast safer

The Cockpit

Perhaps because cockpit design doesn't present the same marketing opportunities as the living space below it, it's not unusual to find that their layouts have been compromised in favour of a commodious after-cabin. This is borne out by a number of modestly sized boats that accept the disadvantages of a centre-cockpit in favour of a veritable bedroom where the cockpit should rightly be. The benefits and disadvantages of centre v. aft cockpit layouts are discussed in the next chapter.

Under way, the cockpit is the centre of activity. Steering, watchkeeping, sail trimming or just plain relaxing – it's all done from here. Sheets, cleats and jammers should fall readily to hand, and winch handles must be able to operate 'full circle'. Properly thought out, it will be a satisfying and safe place to be – efficient for sailors and comfortable for our guests.

Foremost in the designer's mind should be the steering gear. For a wheel-steered yacht a 'T'-shaped cockpit is often the preferred solution, giving the otherwise trapped helmsman room to move around the wheel into the main part of the cockpit. The cockpit seats of a tiller-steered yacht must accommodate the sweep of the tiller without interference, and the tiller itself should be of a height and shape to avoid the knees of a sitting helmsman.

A modern style T-shaped cockpit with twin wheels allows the helm to sit to windward

Wheel, or Tiller?

Who told the marketing men that we all want to steer our boats with wheels? Not me.

Admittedly, centre-cockpit designs have to be wheel steered owing to the distance between the helming position and the rudder. So too do large, heavy-displacement designs where the tiller would need to be inconveniently long.

But for all other designs under 15m or so a tiller often makes more sense, and is much more fun. Nothing beats sitting out on the coaming with a tiller extension, helming the boat like a large dinghy. Well, for a while anyway – gone are the days when I'd do this for hour after hour.

Tillers should be shaped to clear the thighs

When we built *Alacazam*, who responds enthusiastically to this kind of involvement, we positioned the primary and secondary winches a bum-width apart for this very purpose. Strangely, over the years, they've got closer together. Having confessed my preference, perhaps I should explain myself. In an aft-cockpit boat, a tiller:

- Through its direct attachment to the rudder, rewards the helmsman with ultimate feel and feedback
- By virtue of its mechanical simplicity ensures reliability and robustness
- Lets the helmsman, steering with the tiller between his legs, trim the jib, mainsheet and, if he's really brave, the spinnaker without disturbing the off-watch crew
- Works well with both windvane servo-pendulum self-steering gears and electronic autopilots
- Allows the helmsman to gain shelter from the sprayhood
- At anchor can be lifted up out of the way, leaving the cockpit clear
- Can't be geared down, however, to make high steering loads manageable

Whereas a wheel:

- Can be geared down to make high steering loads manageable
- Positions the helmsman right aft, denying him any protection from the sprayhood
- In most cases, doesn't allow the helmsman to trim the sails on his own
- Is less precise than a tiller, and offers the helmsman little feedback
- Requires an expensive and complicated linkage arrangement of wires and blocks, which without regular maintenance is prone to failure
- Is awkward to link to both windvane self-steering gears and electronic autopilots
- Adds weight right aft, just where you need it least
- Clutters up the cockpit when at anchor
- Is expensive

Pointedly, all wheel-steered boats have – or should have – an emergency tiller, which may tell us something. Fashion has a lot to answer for.

Cockpit Ergonomics and Dimensions

The cockpit must feel secure. But it won't if the sensation is of being perched upon on it rather than being in it. Security is largely a function of depth, over which other factors have a controlling influence:

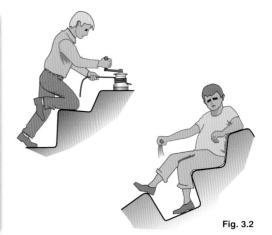

- At extreme angles of heel the leeward edge of the sole must remain above the waterline level to enable it to drain.
- The cockpit sole should not be so deep that it is impossible to see over the coachroof when standing up.
- Although the dimensions of the human body determine the height of the seat above the sole, usually 375mm to 500mm, ideally you'll also be able to see over the coachroof when sitting down.

Fig. 3.2

Other features to be found in a good, sea-going cockpit include:

- Seatbacks that are at least 350mm high and angled so that you can remain sitting upright on the windward side when the boat is heeled
- Seats wide enough, around 500mm, to provide adequate support under the thighs
- Seats that are parallel and close enough together to enable seated occupants on the windward side to brace their feet comfortably against the leeward seats when heeled
- Moderate volume and adequate drainage. For an after cockpit boat, the most efficient drainage is through the transom. A couple of 50mm diameter holes here will drain a moderately sized cockpit inside two minutes
- A bridgedeck to at least the height of the seats, which not only reduces the volume of the cockpit well but also provides a step-up to the companionway sill
- The companionway sill should be at least as high as the coaming, thereby preventing a cockpit full of water from finding its way below
- A main hatch, preferably on the centreline, with moderately angled sides. Washboards in a heavily vee'd hatch only have to float up a short distance before they fall out.

Fig. 3.3

All this talk of cockpit flooding reminds me of a wild night off Cape Trafalgar. I had been waiting in Vilamoura for the easterly Levanter to blow itself out, before continuing my single-handed passage to Gibraltar. When it did, I set off. Within a few hours the fresh easterly wind had increased considerably. Snug in the deep cockpit of my heavy-displacement, long-keeled 32-footer, I looked forward to a fast passage. A while later, with darkness approaching, the wind now howling and some serious-looking seas building up astern, my thoughts turned to slowing *Jalingo* down. Head down in the cockpit locker, searching for the long warp that I kept for such situations, fate chose that moment to try us with a boarding sea. With the cockpit and one of the lockers now largely full of water, and with little chance of it draining through *Jalingo's* pathetic cockpit drains before the next one arrived, I was a little apprehensive as to the immediate future. Clearly I lived to tell the tale, and arrived safely in Gibraltar, but it remains a memorable experience.

Which is why our current boat, *Alacazam*, has no cockpit lockers and two large drainage holes through the transom. We rely on pockets sewn into the back of the cockpit dodgers (weather cloths in the USA) for small items, and a walk-in bosun's locker below, accessed through the heads, for large ones. Shallow lockers with smallish lids were considered, but then the space below would have been less accessible. Incidentally, if you do have cockpit lockers, it's worth securing the raised lid to the guardrails as the following horror story will demonstrate. Perhaps any sufferer of claustrophobia should skip the next paragraph.

Domoi, a Contessa 32, was lying peacefully in a Trinidadian anchorage. Bill, her single-handed Canadian skipper, was kneeling in the cockpit locker, fiddling with the compressor. A powerboat roared past, *Domoi* rocked in its wake, the cockpit lid slammed shut, and the latches flipped over and locked. Bill was now doubled over and trapped in the locker. He was in the dark, airless and oven-like locker for close on half an hour before his desperate shouts for help were heard. Had they not been, the consequences would have been unthinkable – except for Bill, who was thinking about them a lot.

Cockpit lids should be capable of being secured

Protection from the Elements – Sprayhoods, Dodgers and Doghouses

The primary function of a canvas sprayhood is to avoid having to close the main hatch in inclement conditions. While a pramhood type will satisfy this requirement admirably, a more substantial version will contribute greatly to cockpit comfort when the spray starts to fly. But often the comfort aspect is allowed to take undue precedence over the following:

• Restrictions to visibility
• Restrictions to forward access
• Windage
• Aesthetics

A low profile sprayhood that you can see over when standing in the cockpit, and provides space for a crew member to huddle under, is a good compromise. This type can be easily and quickly folded forward out of the way when not needed.

Low profile sprayhoods add very little windage...

High-profile sprayhoods provide the greatest protection, but are often the least successful in terms of the four bullet points above. With this type, you look through its clear plastic screen when standing in the cockpit. What you don't want is the top of the sprayhood at eye level, requiring you to stoop to see under it or stand on tiptoes to peek over it.

Stainless steel grabrails built into the framework provide additional security when going forward, but prevent the sprayhood from being collapsible.

... where towering sprayhoods most certainly do

At anchor in hot weather, and particularly in the tropics, the cooling breeze that might otherwise be enjoyed by cockpit occupants is neatly deflected off them by a fixed sprayhood. Not so much of a problem with a smaller low-profile type, but enough of one for larger versions to need zipped, roll-up windows. These are fine when new, but over a period of time salt and ultra-violet degradation will affect their operation.

Incidentally, Americans call our sprayhoods 'dodgers' and, in an attempt to confuse us further, call our dodgers 'weathercloths'. But we'll not get too hung up about it, and just say that dodgers work in conjunction with the sprayhood in protecting us from the elements, and provide some privacy when at anchor.

Doghouses

These are the ultimate development of a sprayhood. Rigid and robustly constructed, they provide full protection in heavy weather and, with opening windows that don't leak, they are an eminently seaworthy feature. The windows should be of toughened or laminated glass, not acrylic or polycarbonate which will eventually craze or (in the case of polycarbonate) fog. Smoked glass is often used which, although beneficial in strong sunlight, greatly reduces night-time visibility. Some manufacturers – the French-built Amel range for one – go one stage further and include the main steering position (which of course must be a wheel) within the doghouse.

Rigid sprayhoods can't be removed in fair weather

Homebuilt retro-fitted fitted versions, though often of ingenious design, are not always quite so successful from an aesthetic point of view.

Getting On and Off

UK marinas generally provide us with finger berths, which make clambering aboard over the side a fairly straightforward affair. Even so, it can go wrong. Failure to lift your leading leg high enough to clear the top guard wire while lunging for the cap shroud is likely to lead to an ignominious sequence of events, particularly if you're clutching an armful of groceries. A gate in the guard rails, particularly for boats with high freeboards, is a convenient feature.

A wooden plank serves as a simple passarelle

In other parts of the world, and particularly in the Mediterranean, finger berths are a rarity, and stern-to or bow-to mooring is the norm. Stern-to you'll need a passarelle, which is a posh-sounding word for a gang plank. It's French, and means 'footbridge'. The inboard end is attached to the stern and the other rests on the quay, or is supported just above it by an elasticated bridle. An effective passarelle can be made by lashing a plywood plank to an aluminium ladder which, incidentally, is no bad thing to have on board.

I prefer to go bows-to, not just to avoid the risk of damaging the self-steering gear but also to ward off the gaze of promenading pedestrians when relaxing in the cockpit. Often it's possible to get the bow close enough to the quay to be able to step neatly ashore, but there's no doubt that a simple step secured to the pulpit makes boarding easier.

At anchor, a bathing platform makes alighting from the dinghy a simple affair, and a swing-up bathing ladder is essential for swimmers. Providing it's swung down, that is. It's a strange thing, but sailing around with the ladder down and trailing in your wake attracts the same kind of scornful attention from other sailors as leaving your fenders dangling over the side. I've never done that.

Bathing platforms make boarding a boat easy

4

ACCOMMODATION

"We've just bought it," they said. "This very one. It's ours." Clearly delighted with their new acquisition, they beckoned us below.

We were at the boat show, sitting in the aft-cockpit of a purposeful-looking 38ft production cruising boat, and leafing through the brochures the salesman had handed to us. We went below, as invited.

"Two double cabins aft and another forward. A really comfortable saloon, and great for the cook," they said, pointing out the dinette area to starboard, the galley opposite and the diminutive chart table. "We can get eight people around it, and the table drops down to make another double bed. Eight berths in all!" It went on like this – two heads complete with showers, velour upholstery everywhere. "We can't wait to get her in the water," they said. "Weekends cruising along the south coast with our friends and both sets of kids. They just love Poole Harbour. In the summer holidays we'll head further west, Dartmouth, Salcombe, Plymouth, Fowey, Falmouth, or maybe the Channel Islands if the weather's settled."

I was about to point out that the prospect of sailing anywhere on a 38ft boat with seven other people didn't exactly fill me with joy, when realisation dawned – closely followed by relief that my criticism of the boat's apparent shortcomings had remained unspoken. This boat wasn't supposed to be an offshore cruiser – it just looked like one from the outside. It was a family boat intended for harbour-hopping with only an occasional night spent at sea – never far from onshore facilities where its systems could be plugged in and topped up. Just perfect for the use to which the new owners would put it – a veritable sailing caravan.

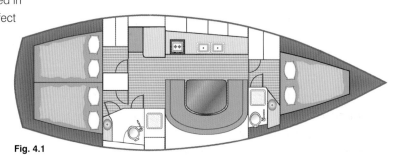

Fig. 4.1

At least I hope that's what the designer's intentions were – otherwise he'd got it seriously wrong. But, had this boat been intended for offshore sailing, how would its interior have differed?

- The primary difference would be that it wouldn't be designed to cater for the requirements of eight people. Four would be an ideal crew, although the boat could easily (and most likely would) be handled by two people. In my experience most long-distance cruising boats are crewed by a cruising couple, occasionally supplemented by one or two others when on a potentially arduous ocean passage.
- The two double berths aft rule out all but the most meagre of cockpit lockers. One of the double berths could be retained; the other converted to a bosun's locker for storing warps, fenders, sails, the dinghy, outboard motor and so on, accessed through the heads.
- The double vee berth forward would serve better as two single berths, with a separate infill piece for use should the forecabin occupants be (or become) closely acquainted.
- The berths in the after and forecabin will be fine for in-harbour use, but not so when under way. Single sea berths must be provided for the off-watch crew. More on this below, but if the saloon seating is to be utilised for these, it's goodbye to the curved seating in the dinette area. In any event curved seating is seldom successful on sailboats – a progressively smaller length of it remaining comfortable (or even tenable) as the boat heels.

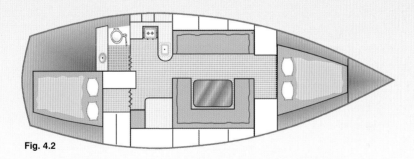

Fig. 4.2

- Calculating the loo/crew ratio to avert a conflict in times of dire need is an exercise in probability assessment, but by my reckoning more than one head in a boat of this size is a ludicrous waste of space. There's only one sensible location for the heads – aft, at the foot of the companionway. Anywhere else, then in bad weather a wet, dripping, oilskin-clad crew member will have to traipse right through the accommodation to get to it.
- With the two heads taking up the most stable part of the boat, the only place left for the designer to put the galley is forward in the saloon. In hot weather, and with any kind of sea running, the cook won't thank him for this. A more practical location for the galley is further aft, next to the companionway.

Sleeping Around

Berths can be broadly divided into two types; those that can only be utilised when the boat is flat and level, and those that are also suitable for use in a seaway. All doubles fall into the former category (unless divided by a longitudinal lee cloth) along with forepeak berths on account of the pitching motion in the forward part of the boat.

Sea berths in cruising boats are normally one of the following types:

- Settee berths which, as the name suggests, are the seats for sitting at the cabin table. Often they can be pulled out by a few inches when in bunk mode to create more width for the slumbering occupant.
- Pilot berths, which are permanent berths outboard and above the settee backs. These are probably the best bunks of all for daytime sleeping as they don't interfere with the normal use of the cabin. Unfortunately, smaller boats probably won't have sufficient beam for them.

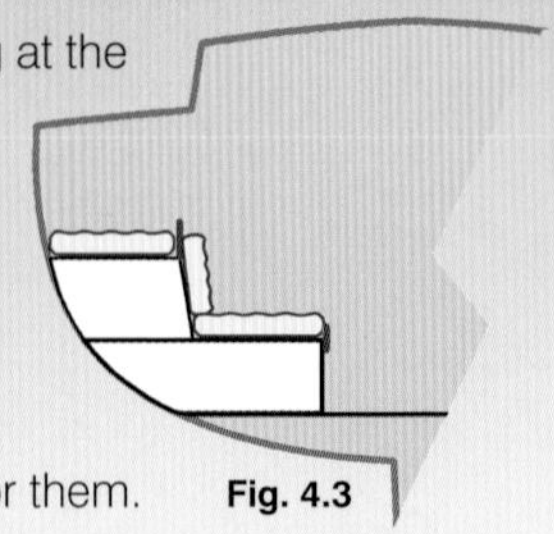

Fig. 4.3

- Quarter berths, which are located under the outboard edge of the cockpit. While out of the way of cabin traffic, they tend to be poorly ventilated and can be particularly hot and noisy when under power. Getting in and out of them requires a degree of gymnastic ability.

The fundamental design features of a good sea berth are:

- It should be parallel to the centreline of the yacht as is practicable. Otherwise, the occupant will find himself head-down on one tack and head-up on the other – neither attitude being conducive to a decent kip.
- For comfort and security the ideal width is 700mm to 750mm, with 600mm as the absolute minimum. Pilot berths and settee berths must be fitted with lee cloths or bunk boards to keep the occupants snugly in place when the boat is heeling and rolling. A lee cloth should have a gap of around 500mm at the occupant's head for ventilation.
- The minimum length of the berth should be 2m, which would allow a conventionally proportioned adult to use a pillow.

On a shorthanded boat, there's much to be said for a dedicated sea berth at the foot of the companionway. If the berth cushions are covered in waterproof fabric, a wet and exhausted crew can nap here – even in his foul-weather gear – until roused from his slumbers by a hearty shout from the cockpit. On *Alacazam* we've sacrificed a sit-down navigation area in favour of such a berth, and a good compromise it's turned out to be, with all the key facilities – galley, heads, navigation area and sea berth – located at the foot of the companionway.

A Seagoing Galley

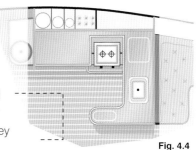

Fig. 4.4

Some people enjoy cooking – I don't. Eating's more my thing. Anyone who can conjure up a nourishing meal on a pitching, rolling boat is a treasure beyond value and should be cherished unreservedly. And anything that can be done to make his or her life easier is likely to bring rich culinary rewards. An efficient galley is a good place to start.

The location should be well ventilated and easily accessible to both the cockpit and the saloon. The common arrangement is for it to be at the foot of the companionway, and this has much in its favour. This part of the boat is less prone to violent pitching, there's good natural ventilation through the companionway and hot food and drinks may be easily passed up to the cockpit. There's not a lot you can do about the rolling, but the cooker should be gimballed on its longitudinal access, which will largely take care of that.

Some centre-cockpit boats have a linear galley in the passageway linking the aftcabin to the rest of the boat, on the basis that there's not much else you can do with the space. This is a less successful arrangement than those that have an L-shaped galley with the cooker and sinks in the conventional place, and only the work tops and refrigerator tucked into the passageway.

The cooking process, for those of you that aren't familiar with it, produces a deal of steam and heat which will create condensation and encourage the dreaded mildew. An opening portlight or extractor fan above the galley will go a long way to relieving this unwanted side effect, if the ventilation provided by the companionway is insufficient.

The three main units – cooker, sinks and refrigerator – should be close together so that the cook can reach all three without having to move more than a step or two, which is more easily achieved with a U-shaped or L-shaped galley than the linear arrangement.

Restrained - or constrained?

A restraining harness should be rigged to secure the cook in close to the cooker when it's to windward, and there should be a stout metal bar across the front of the cooker to keep the cook from accidentally falling onto it when it's to leeward. But beware! When secured by the harness, the cook has nowhere to go if he/she spills a pan of hot liquid, and many serious scalds have occurred this way. In boisterous conditions, it's a sound idea to wear a full-length waterproof apron, or the lower half of your foulies.

There should be adequate work tops with high (75mm), sturdy fiddles, and a heatproof area to put down a hot pan. Stainless steel sheet should be fixed to protect adjacent cabinetry and the hull side outboard of the cooker, as these surfaces can get very hot.

Stainless steel dual sinks – one for washing, the other for draining – should be deep enough (150mm to 200mm) to retain plates, and to prevent spillage when the boat rolls.

Centre Cockpits and Aftcabins

A pal of mine once had a boat show salesman speechless when being led into the aftcabin (sorry – 'the owner's stateroom') of a 14m cruising boat. "Good Lord," he said. "It's a fornicatorium!" I know what he meant. A king-sized walk-around bed with en-suite facilities – it would've stood comparison with an upmarket honeymoon-hotel bedroom.

It can provide a level of privacy and seclusion not normally found on a sailboat – an in-harbour refuge par excellence – separated from the rest of the accommodation by a walk-through passageway. But a separate aftcabin only works on larger boats, where there's enough room outboard or beneath the cockpit to allow access into it from the accommodation. On smaller centre-cockpit boats with separate aftcabins, access is through a forward-facing companionway leading from the cockpit, which is not good for three reasons:

- Facing into the elements, this type of companionway is very wet in bad weather
- When the companionway is left open to the cockpit, as it must be to provide light and ventilation, the occupants have almost no privacy if other people are aboard
- It's too remote from the rest of the accommodation. Shut away in the cabin, what chance is there of hearing the anchor chain graunch in the stemhead when the boat drags its anchor?

Doors or Curtains?

I once had a boat with the heads located forward of the saloon. There was no room for a conventional door, so the builder had fitted an athwartship sliding door to close it off from the saloon. If you forgot to secure it properly it would slam across on a tack and either jam or fall off its runners, both of which came as something of a surprise to anyone enthroned within. It was a hopeless and completely unnecessary arrangement. I took it off and replaced it with a curtain, which worked perfectly. We carried this thinking forward when *Alacazam* was built. Now we have no doors, just curtains. They never jam, they're light, don't get in the way, allow ventilation from stem to stern, don't need painting or varnishing and can be easily cleaned or cheaply replaced.

Curtains are lighter, offer better ventilation and don't rattle

SELF-STEERING

I enjoy helming a sailboat. Sitting out on the cockpit coaming, tiller extension in one hand, telltales streaming nicely. It's exhilarating – all that power under your direct control. But not for long – and in inclement conditions not at all if I can avoid it. Some form of self-steering is essential for an offshore boat. There are three ways of achieving it:

• Windvane self-steering   • Electronic autopilot   • Sheet to tiller steering

So before we look at them in detail, what are the main strengths and weaknesses of these different approaches?

	Strengths	Weaknesses
Windvane Gear	Uses no electricity. Mechanically robust, reliable and easily maintained. Steers to the apparent wind direction, no need for constant sail trimming.	If wind shifts, you change course. Doesn't work under power. Initially expensive. Steering lines cross cockpit with servopendulum types. Weight on stern. Won't work on multihulls.
Electronic Autopilot	Push-button operation. Can be interfaced with other electronic instruments, giving the option of steering to wind, compass heading or a defined route. Works under sail or power.	Uses electricity. Can be unreliable. Complex and difficult (at best) to repair. Doesn't distinguish between monos and multihulls.
Sheet to tiller	Uses no electricity. If you can get it to work, it's the ultimate in simplicity.	Difficult to set up initially. Won't work on all points of sail. Won't work with wheel steering.

Windvane Self-steering

Not so long ago you could differentiate a boat intended for long offshore passages from its coastal cousin by the windvane gear bolted to the transom, but this is no longer true. Many offshore sailors now opt for a compact and discreet electronic system instead – which is a shame, as there's an elegant simplicity in the workings of a windvane.

Essentially, these entirely mechanical devices sense the apparent wind direction and steer the boat on a course relative to it. The apparent wind, a concept familiar to all sailors, is the wind we feel when standing on deck. Only if the boat is stationary will the true wind be the same as the apparent wind.

For a brief refresher, let's imagine a stationary boat with a 10-knot wind on the beam. As the boat moves ahead the apparent wind will move forward of the beam and increase in strength.

Windvane self-steering gear linked to the tiller by two simple lines

A further increase in boat speed will bring the wind further ahead and increase its apparent speed. These changes will be sensed by the masthead wind direction indicator, which will align with the apparent wind – and the windvane will react in exactly the same manner. To carry this scenario to the extreme, if the vessel was a racing trimaran creaming along at 20 knots then it would effectively be close-hauled, although still sailing on a beam reach. So it can readily be appreciated that the factors affecting apparent wind are:

- True wind speed
- True wind direction
- Boat's course relative to the true wind direction
- Boat's speed over the ground

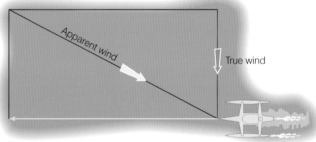

Fig. 5.1

The wind is never constant. It gusts, veers and backs, each of which will cause a change in apparent wind, to which the windvane reacts with a course change.

But as the sails are trimmed to the relative wind, the boat continues to sail efficiently, the heading being continually adjusted as if by an expert helmsman.

When the actual course deviates from the desired course to the extent that it's necessary to do something about it, then a gentle tweak of the course adjustment line and some sail trimming gets everything, well, back on course.

So how do vane-gears work? Put simply, the windvane senses the apparent wind, then through a linkage to either the boat's own rudder or a separate auxiliary rudder adjusts the boat's course relative to the apparent wind. So let's take a look at these three elements – windvane, linkage and rudder – in turn.

The Windvane

The steering impulse is generated by the apparent wind flowing across the surface of the windvane. The simplest windvanes are made of marine ply, so it's easy to produce a few spares – but it's important that these are cut to the same shape as the manufacturer's design, and absolutely vital that they're within prescribed weight tolerances. Other materials used are plastic, aluminium and synthetic fabric stretched over a metal frame. There are two types of windvane: those that pivot around a vertical axis, and those that pivot around a horizontal axis.

Vertical axis windvanes rotate about their leading edge, much like a weathercock, and always point directly into the wind. Consequently, the vane area responding to the action of the wind is relatively small. A counterbalance is fixed ahead of the axis to prevent gravity deflecting the windvane when the boat heels. When the boat wanders off course the windvane is deflected by the same angle as the off-course deviation. The corrective steering energy generated by this deflection is small, owing to the negligible torque generated by vertical axis windvanes.

Horizontal axis windvanes rotate about their lower edge, and are counterbalanced such that, in a no-wind condition or when facing edge-on directly into the wind, they will stand upright until deflected from that condition. When the boat wanders off course and the wind strikes the windvane from one side, it tilts over, exposing the whole of one face to the force of the wind. As a result it has a substantially larger effective area than the vertical axis windvanes. Horizontal axis windvanes are therefore able to exert considerably more leverage than vertical axis windvanes and are said to be over five times as efficient.

In practice, the axes of such vanes aren't horizontal but are inclined at an angle of about 20°. This is to counteract the characteristic of truly horizontal vanes to slam hard over from side to side, producing a correspondingly dramatic effect on the steering. By inclining the axis, the vane's power diminishes as it's pushed over (see fig. 5.2), producing a much more sensitive steering effect.

Fig. 5.2

The Linkage

There are several ways of transmitting the steering impulse from the windvane to the rudder. They include bevel gears, pushrods and sheathed push-pull cables. This latter method allows the windvane to be positioned to avoid dinghy davits and the like, which may otherwise preclude the use of a vane-gear system. The Auto-Helm® is an example of the cable operated type.

Apart from direct action gears like the Hydrovane®, where the vane operates its own rudder, most gears use some form of servo effect. Perhaps the simplest example is where a trim-tab (in effect a relatively tiny rudder) is fitted to the main rudder blade. The windvane alters the angle of tab and the waterflow acting upon it pushes the rudder blade to one side. It could be said that the tab steers the rudder and the rudder steers the boat.

Much more powerful are what are known as 'pendulum servo' gears. On these, the windvane turns a high aspect ratio blade which is swept to one side or other by the waterflow. At any sort of speed, the power generated by this action is awesome. Its action is harnessed by steering lines which are led back to the tiller or wheel.

Most gears employ one or other of these servo mechanisms, sometimes even combining the two in the same unit.

Feedback

Early windvane gears – particularly the super-powerful pendulum servo gears – could be quite violent in their actions and it became necessary to dampen their excesses by introducing some form of corrective feedback into the linkage geometry. There are various ways of achieving this but an easily understood example can be demonstrated by looking at a simple trim-tab gear (Fig 5.3). By having the trim-tab arm pivot behind the rudder's axis, the action of the tab gradually reduces to become zero as the rudder blade turns.

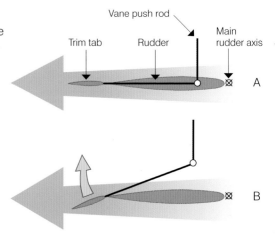

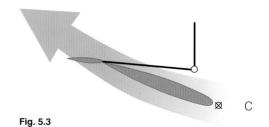

With the boat on course (A) the trim tab has a neutral effect but any deviation from the course (B) is sensed by the windwave which applies corrective action. Because the trim tab's control point is behind the rudder's axis (C), as the rudder swings over it progressively negates the trim tab's effect.

Fig. 5.3

So, let's look at the various types:

Direct action with auxiliary rudder: These are self-contained units where the vane directly operates its own rudder with no servo effects being employed. The Hydrovane® is by far the best known of this type.

Servo tab on main rudder: One of the oldest and simplest forms of self-steering and probably the least sensitive. It should be noted that the action of the tab first steers the boat the 'wrong' way – that's to say, its immediate effect before the rudder turns is to promote the yaw further.

Servo tab on auxiliary rudder: Another self-contained arrangement. The main rudder is usually trimmed then lashed to compensate for any helm bias, leaving the self-steering gear to correct minor course deviations. One drawback with this arrangement is that the auxiliary rudder is relatively small and may not be sufficiently powerful to bring the boat back from being violently thrown off course.

Pendulum servo on auxiliary rudder: Here, a servo blade operates its own rudder, dispensing with the need for steering lines. It shares the limitations of the previous type, with the notable exception that the pendulum blade contributes to the steering effect.

Pendulum servo acting on main rudder: Comfortably the most powerful type. However, the steering lines must be led to the tiller or wheel, which can be awkward on centre-cockpit boats. Since it's the main rudder that actually does the steering, it doesn't suffer the shortcomings of auxiliary rudder types.

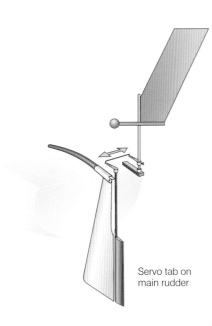

Servo tab on main rudder

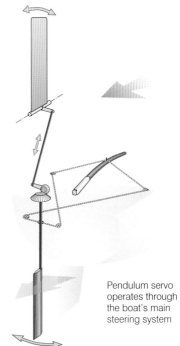

Pendulum servo operates through the boat's main steering system

Fig. 5.4

	Strengths	Weaknesses
Servopendulum systems	Steering forces increase with wind speed and vessel speed. Rudders can be removed when not in use. Works directly on main steering. Usually some form of collision damage protection built in.	Steering lines to helm can clutter cockpit. Not readily suited for use as an emergency rudder.
Auxiliary Rudder systems	Can be used as an emergency steering system in the event of main rudder failure. No steering lines in cockpit. Trim-tab models more sensitive than servopendulums in light airs. Better alternative for centre-cockpits and hydraulic steering.	Less steering power than servopendulums. Permanent installation, susceptible to collision damage. Affects steering when moving astern under power.

Electronic Autopilots

If your batteries can keep up with an electronic autopilot's appetite for electricity, then for short-distance sailing they make an attractive alternative to windvane self-steering. Most autopilots – and certainly the simplest ones – steer to a compass course, but more sophisticated models can be interfaced with the wind direction indicator, thus responding to windshifts in the same way as windvanes. Many offshore sailors carry both a windvane and autopilot – the latter to steer the boat under power when the electrical supply should be plentiful.

There are two basic types: a cockpit tiller (or wheel) autopilot, and an inboard type working directly (and usually unseen) on the primary steering mechanism. Both types have fluxgate compasses to guide them.

Cockpit Tiller Autopilots

These are the simplest form of autopilot, in which an electric motor is connected via a transmission directly to a push rod. The push rod extends or retracts to move the tiller. Small tiller pilots, suitable for boats up to around 4,500kg displacement, consist of a single module which includes the compass, the control unit, the motor and push rod.

In larger models, suitable for boats up to around 7,500kg displacement, the control unit and compass are separate modules. All tiller autopilots tend to be a little noisy – rather like the distant yapping of a small dog.

Cockpit Wheel Autopilots

These are very similar to the tiller version, except that course corrections are applied to the wheel by a belt, rather than a pushrod.

In recent years the trend towards system integration has extended to include those cockpit autopilots that have a separate control/display unit. To get the most out of such units you need to integrate them with a compatible GPS or chartplotter, and a wind instrument either mounted at the masthead or at the stern of the boat. This gives three main operating modes:

- Auto: the autopilot is locked onto a heading.
- Track: the autopilot is locked onto a track between two waypoints.
- Windvane: the autopilot maintains a course relative to the apparent wind. However, in practice, if there's much of a swell running, neither a masthead instrument nor a stern-mounted one will give a particularly satisfactory result. The masthead unit will suffer from the motion of the boat, and a stern-mounted unit will be operating in a disturbed airflow. The resulting impulses have to be damped and processed to obtain a useful signal.

All sorts of data display and functionality are now available on the display unit – cross-track error, off-course alarm, waypoint proximity alarm, windshift alarm and so on. One very useful trick is 'Autotack', initiated by some judicious button-pressing. Great news for a short-handed crew, who can now deal with the sails while the autopilot is putting the boat about.

Inboard Autopilot

An inboard autopilot can do all of the clever stuff mentioned above and lots more, usually being fully integrated with the boat's navigational system. They're much more powerful than the cockpit versions, suitable for large sailing boats and power boats, and a deal more expensive as a result. Instead of connection to a tiller or wheel, they use push rods or hydraulic systems connected to the rudder post (or quadrant) to turn the main rudder directly.

Power consumption of an electronic autopilot can be significant, the key factors affecting it being:

- Sail trim: poorly trimmed sails and excessive weather helm.
- Sea state: bigger seas and increased yawing require more frequent steering adjustments.
- Autopilot setting: the more precise the course setting, the greater the work to be done by the autopilot.
- Boat displacement and length: the more boat there is to move, the greater the work to be done by the autopilot.
- Underwater shape: notwithstanding the tracking properties of a long-keeler, a keel-mounted rudder will require more force because it's impossible to balance, whereas a fully balanced spade rudder will be lightest on the helm.

Synergy Between a Tiller Pilot and a Vane Gear

Isn't it just great when this happens? By removing the windvane from a vane-gear and connecting a small tiller autopilot in its place you can now use your vane-gear when under power. The pendulum or trim-tab now works with the autopilot, greatly reducing power consumption. Some vane-gears, like the Auto-Helm® and the Windpilot® Pacifics, for example, are constructed with this in mind and have the connection fitting built in. Some manufacturers don't recommend it because the turbulent wake can damage the pendulum blade bearings.

Sheet to Tiller Self-Steering

Few of us would set out on a long offshore passage relying solely on a sheet-to-tiller steering, but when all else fails...

As far as I'm aware there's no prescribed way to set it up so it will work in any set of conditions. As the point of sailing changes, or the wind pipes up or falls away, then you've some serious tweaking of the lines and blocks to do. Tacking and gybing can be a fun time too. It's very much trial and error, and it's well worth experimenting before you're caught well offshore with an electronic autopilot that's withdrawn its support. That's what an American sailor, John F. Letcher Jr, spent a lot of his time doing in the 1960s and 1970s, so much so that he wrote a book – *Self-Steering for Sailing Craft* – on the subject. JFL Jr recognised that most sailboats are designed so that the helm is balanced in light air, but as the wind gusts, the boat heels and weatherhelm increases. Most boats then tend to round up into the wind, requiring the helmsman to pull the tiller up to windward to keep the boat on course. By connecting the sheet to the tiller through a system of lines and blocks, the theory is that the increase in the sheet load will do what the helmsman would otherwise have to do. A bungee cord attached to the tiller opposing the load of the sheet gets everything back together as the weatherhelm decreases.

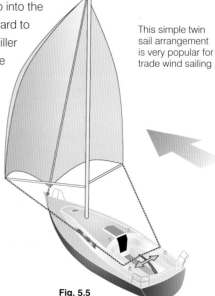

This simple twin sail arrangement is very popular for trade wind sailing

Fig. 5.5

WATER SUPPLY & CONSERVATION

In the days of wooden boats and iron men – where personal hygiene wasn't quite so high on the list of priorities – the fresh water provision for a voyage was calculated on the basis of half a gallon per person per day, with something in reserve for emergencies. Proposing this to your crew today is unlikely to be well received – at least double that would be the expectation.

Planning a 3,000-mile hop across to the West Indies with a crew of four, the skipper of a 40ft (12.2m) yacht would probably allow for a 25-day passage (although he might reasonably expect to make the crossing in less than 20) and, at 1 gallon (2.6L) per person per day, choose to start off with 100 gallons (261L) in his tanks. Many 40-footers won't have this capacity in their built-in tanks, so an additional flexible tank may have to be installed, or a number of plastic jerrycans carried. It's clearly a mistake to start off with insufficient water for the entire duration of the passage, relying on a watermaker or raincatcher to make up the deficit.

Ideally, the water should be stowed in two separate tanks to avoid the risk of cross-contamination. There can be a 'balance pipe' between them but this should only be opened during filling. In this arrangement, the risk of cross-contamination is avoided and, provided the valves in the balance pipe are only opened during filling, a failure in one tank won't drain the other. A 'Y' valve on the distribution side enables you to draw water from either tank.

As recently as 20 years ago few boats had pressurised water, all of it being drawn from the tanks by foot pumps or hand pumps. A separate seawater pump at the galley for washing dishes was the norm.

You would only pump as much water as needed, and little wastage occurred as a result. You had your shower when it rained, and washed your clothes by towing them astern in a net bag for an hour or so, then rinsing the salt out in rainwater – a method that still works.

Modern cruising boats do little to encourage the prudent use of water. Pressurised hot and cold water will be on tap not only in the showers, but also at the galley sink and in the wash-hand basins. Just like at home – and all very nice it is too, providing you can carry, collect, or produce sufficient water to satiate their demand, and generate enough electricity to keep it all going.

The output from a pressurised shower is staggering, as I discovered when I checked *Alacazam's* cockpit shower. A five-second squirt into a measuring jug produced 675ml – equivalent to 97 gallons per hour. I can shower away my daily allowance in 37 seconds flat and empty my tanks completely in an hour or so. Clearly this beast demands respect when far from a source of water replenishment, when a wise skipper may well switch it off altogether, extolling the virtues of a flannel and an inch or two of water in a small bowl. For the less prescriptive, a manually pressurised spray bottle or a solar shower bag could provide an acceptably conservative alternative – once a week or so.

Clearly, on a long ocean passage it's vital to monitor water consumption, not just to discover how much of it has gone, but more importantly to ascertain if and how consumption should be adjusted to avoid running out before the end of the voyage.

The calculation should be made on the basis that the watermaker will fail, and there'll be no further rainfall. All offshore yachts should have a manual system installed alongside the pressurised one (that can be switched off) for use on passage when more frugal water consumption becomes necessary. In particular, a foot pump at the galley will leave your hands free and let you get at the water when the electric pump is disabled.

A mid-Atlantic solar shower for the skipper

Water Heaters

Just occasionally – free lunches excepted – you really do get something for nothing; and you should take advantage of it. A sailing boat that uses its engine fairly regularly produces hot water as a by-product of the combustion process, and it's free. You'll need the equipment though – in this case a calorifier. This device is effectively an insulated heat exchanger which, plumbed into the engine cooling water system will transfer heat from the engine into the domestic water supply. A typical hot and cold domestic water installation is shown in fig. 6.1. This system incorporates both a pump and an accumulator. Most water pressure pumps maintain steady pressure by cycling on and off, producing a pulsed delivery. The accumulator tank containing water and air – usually but not always separated by a diaphragm – absorbs this pulsation and provides steady flow. Some pump manufacturers (Jabsco for one) now produce microprocessor-controlled variable-speed pumps which eliminate cycling and make the accumulator tank redundant. The blender valve operates thermostatically, introducing a metered amount of cold water into the outlet flow, thus maintaining regulated temperature and conserving hot water. Of course, if you haven't run the engine for an hour or two, turning on the hot tap won't produce the desired result.

Outlets

Very hot water

Mixer valve

Accumulator

Water tank

Stopcock

Warm water

Filter Pump

Cold water

Hot water from engine

Fig. 6.1

Electric immersion heaters, much like the larger versions we're accustomed to at home, require AC power, so unless you've got a generator aboard their use is restricted to when you're alongside and hooked-up to an onshore supply. Immersion heaters are often combined with a calorifier in a single unit.

Watermakers

Osmosis is a word guaranteed to raise the pulse rate of most boat owners. Defined as 'the diffusion of fluid through a semi-permeable membrane from a solution with a low solute concentration to a solution with a higher solute concentration until there's an equal concentration of fluid on both sides of the membrane', it's the most likely cause of the blisters that sometimes appear below the waterline on GRP boats.

Alacazam's 1 gallon per hour watermaker installation

The diffusion takes place only if the liquids either side of the membrane are of differing solute concentrations, and the transfer is always from the least to the most concentrated side. In this context, the semi-permeable membrane is the gelcoat, through which the water has diffused to mix with the more highly concentrated liquids – undissolved resins, solvents and the like – contained in minute quantities in the laminate on the other, to produce the dreaded blisters.

Reverse osmosis is a filtration process achieved by forcing a solvent from a region of high-solute concentration through a semi-permeable membrane to a region of low-solute concentration by applying a pressure in excess of the osmotic pressure. While it's sadly not a corrective repair option for blistered hulls, it is a convenient way of obtaining drinking water from seawater.

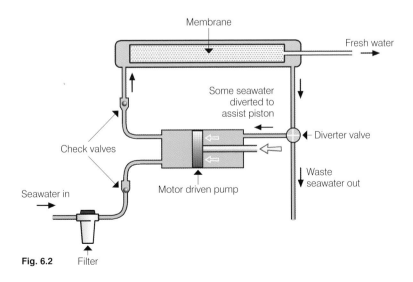

Fig. 6.2

Watermakers designed for yachts use reverse osmosis technology. An electric pump (or in some high-output units a belt-driven one off the engine) forces seawater through a very fine membrane at high pressure, leaving the salt and other impurities on one side and allowing only clean fresh water to emerge from the other. Marine watermakers are designed to process clean, open-ocean seawater. Any departure from that standard of cleanliness is likely to cause damage to the membrane or produce contaminated fresh water. They like to be run often, so they only really come into their own on long offshore passages, or protracted cruising in clean waters. If they're not used at least once a week, then they need to be treated with a biocide to prevent bacterial growth building up on the filter membrane. In the tropics, bacterial growth will be more rapid, and the watermaker will have to be used every couple of days or so if it's to produce good-quality drinking water.

Contrary to what you may expect, the plumbing involved in installing a watermaker doesn't have to involve additional thru-hull fittings; existing pipes can be utilised to supply the raw water intake, dispose the waste water, and deliver the desalinated water to the tanks.

For example, on *Alacazam* the intake is tee'd off the seawater intake to the toilet, the waste water is tee'd into the wash-hand basin waste pipe, and the product line is tee'd into the supply to the wash-hand basin, where it will find its way back to the tanks, as shown in fig. 6.2.

There are four main types of unit available, with outputs from around one gallon an hour to over sixty:

- 12/24v DC
- 110/220v AC, driven by a generator or inverter
- Belt-driven off the main engine
- Towed version

With one of the higher-output versions, pressurised showers and even plumbed-in washing machines can be used with impunity. Not surprisingly, the higher the output, the higher the wattage of the seawater pump. We use a low-output version, a 12v Katadyne Survivor 40e, which draws just 4 amps and produces about 5.7 litres of good-quality drinking water per hour. Our solar panels and wind-generator can easily keep up with its meagre electrical appetite and, run every day, the fresh water output is sufficient for two people, and we only need to biocide the membrane when we lay up. So we turn solar and wind energy into water and, from an environmental point of view, feel pretty smug about it.

It's worth bearing in mind that water produced through reverse osmosis doesn't have the mineral content that our bodies require.

Rainwater Catchment

It would be silly not to. Clean fresh water from the sky, and it's free.

Under way, a bucket slung on the end of the boom is supposed to catch rain water as it pours off the mainsail. In practice, I've found that the motion of the boat prematurely empties it, or the bucket falls off. Many long-distance sailors utilise their biminis and, at anchor, their sun awnings for this purpose. Others make up fabric raincatchers specifically for the purpose, supported by the shrouds and spars. One of these, properly tensioned so that the wind won't throw it all out, can fill your tanks in a couple of hours in a tropical downpour. Provided the first few gallons of water are discarded and the fabric is sluiced clean of any salt, insects or by-products of over-flying birds, then the water is normally clean enough to drink. Depending on your level of confidence in its cleanliness, the water can be either plumbed directly into your tanks, or collected in plastic containers. I choose the latter approach, treating the contents to a water purification tablet – as rainwater will otherwise grow bacteria rather quickly – before transferring it to *Alacazam's* tanks. Other skippers say it's necessary to have several filters in the rainwater catchment system and to keep that water in a separate tank, even then only drinking it after boiling.

The primary filter can be something as simple as a coffee filter or piece of cheese cloth, which will keep any larger solids from passing through. The second should be between the rain water tank and the pump. This should be a standard household-type fresh water filter with a 5 micron filter or so. The third should be a carbon filter between the pump and the tap.

Without a watermaker or raincatcher, you'll have to resort to frequent trips ashore with the jerry cans, or to taking the yacht alongside from time to time. But water can be scarce in many parts of the world, particularly during the dry season, so it seems a little discourteous to expect the local people to share their limited supply with you. We should be self-sufficient wherever we can.

Whatever the source of your water, a battery-powered water tester (such as the Liquatec PM-3000 TDS Pocket Meter) can be used to assess its purity by measuring the Total Dissolved Solids (TDS) in Parts per Million (PM). But a TDS meter works by measuring the electrical conductivity of water. Therefore, it's only able to measure dissolved substances that are ionized in solution, such as sea salt for example. Specifically, it will not indicate the presence of non-ionized substances such as bacteria, viruses or soluble chemicals.

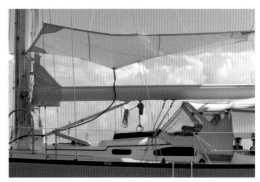

A large purpose-made rain catcher

7

CREW COMFORT

We're a strange bunch, we sailors. We intentionally, and voluntarily, put ourselves in a cold wet environment and then contrive various methods of keeping warm and dry. We dream of tropical seas, warm winds and hot, sunny weather and, having achieved the dream, seek shade and cool breezes.

But whether we're shivering in the North Sea in January or perspiring in the Caribbean in June, adequate ventilation below decks is essential for a comfortable living environment.

Ventilation

This isn't just a comfort issue; it's one of safety too. The ventilation system must provide a through-flow of air at a comfortable temperature and level of humidity to rid the boat not just of unpleasant odours from the galley, the heads and our sweaty bodies but also of noxious fumes produced by the stove, the engine and the batteries. To do so effectively in varying degrees of heat and cold, wind, waves and spray, the system must be flexible and well thought through. The basic principle is that fresh air must be brought in at one end of the boat and let out at the other, without bringing spray or rain with it. The key part of the system is the main companionway, which acts as an exhaust for air brought in from forward or, with the sprayhood up and the breeze aft, an inlet to scoop air below.

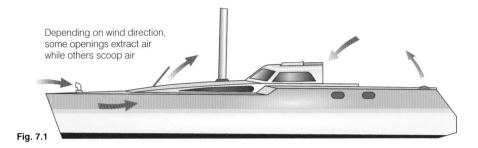

Depending on wind direction, some openings extract air while others scoop air

Fig. 7.1

Other components of the system include:

- **Hatches and portlights:** These serve as both inlets and exhausts, depending on wind direction. If fitted with a small canvas hood they may be left open a few inches to let in air while keeping a rain shower at bay. At sea, except perhaps in the most benign conditions, they should be kept firmly closed.

- **Dorade vents:** So named because of their use by Olin and Rod Stevens on their famous yawl *Dorade* in the 1930s, these cowl vents separate air from water, and can be left open at sea to provide air below. They're not foolproof, however – a malicious sea can find a way below if so inclined – but a screw-in cover can be fitted from below to seal them off. It's important that they're located close to the centreline, as fitted outboard they would be at risk of being flooded in heavy weather. They're effective sheet traps on deck, so some means of preventing this happening should be devised.

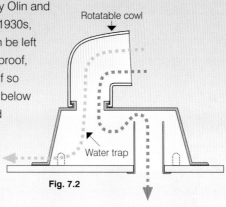

Rotatable cowl

Water trap

Fig. 7.2

- **Baffled vents:** Similar in concept to the dorade vent, but of simpler design and less efficient as a result. They are best used in drier parts of the deck. They're also efficient sheet-trappers and toe-stubbers.

- **Low-profile vents:** These won't trap sheets or stub toes, but can pull in enough air to help ventilate a small cabin. Ideal for the heads, some types are fitted with a solar-driven fan and can be switched to either inlet or exhaust.

- **Mushroom vents:** Also known as a clamshell vent, these tilt-top devices are operated from below, and are often used over the galley stove. Like the low-profile vents, some models are fitted with a solar-operated fan.

- **12v fans:** When there's little breeze to stir the ventilation system into action these will efficiently move the air around below. Some oscillate, which helps the process, and some are quite noisy, which is irritating. I use the twin-blade versions made by Cafrano which are quiet, shift a lot of air and draw only 0.59 amps. The blades are made of a light plastic.

In fair weather it's not difficult to ventilate the boat properly. But in poor conditions offshore with the crew huddled below and the boat closed down, it's a different matter. In such a situation, it's only the dorade vents that can supply the crew with the fresh air that they need without bringing water below.

Air Conditioning

Air conditioners are essentially refrigerators, but instead of retaining the cooled air in an insulated box, it's ducted around the boat and vented out into the areas requiring cooling. Unlike a fridge, however, boats are not enclosed in 100mm-thick insulation, so the cooled air rapidly warms – and escapes through ports and hatches, unless the boat's closed up completely. The only solution to this is to keep producing more of the cold stuff, a process which consumes lots of electricity.

I'll come clean on this one and say it – I wouldn't have an air-conditioning system on my boat as a gift, and think that anyone who would is rather missing the point and would be better off in a hotel.

Very occasionally though, laid up alongside in hot, humid, airless conditions with the wind scoop collapsed lifeless over the forehatch and the cabin fans doing their inadequate best to make sleep even remotely possible in the sauna-like conditions below, I've been heard to mutter, "What I'd give for air conditioning."

Some years ago, while waiting for parts in Chagauramus, Trinidad we found ourselves in just such a situation. Belatedly, we tried to hire an external unit that would fit over a hatch. No luck – we checked into a hotel.

Cabin Heating

For all but the hardiest of UK-based sailors, some form of cabin heating is essential if your boat is to be enjoyed year round. It's not just for the warmth, but also to dispel the dampness that can pervade our boats in cold weather. Cabin heaters fall into two distinct groups:

- Direct heating, where a stand-alone heater disperses warmth through the cabin by natural convection and radiation alone, and
- indirect heating, where heat from a remotely located unit is distributed throughout the boat by ducted hot air or hot-water radiators, much like a domestic central heating system.

There are options within each group. Let's take a look at them:

Direct Heating – Paraffin Fuelled

I once owned a boat with a paraffin-fuelled Taylor cabin heater fitted in the saloon. It threw out great quantities of dry heat for a miserly usage of fuel. It was simple to maintain and, providing I did so regularly, was never any trouble. But the previous owner had installed it halfway up a bulkhead at the forward end of the saloon; there was just nowhere else for it to go. As a result, my lower extremities would still be in the early stages of thawing out while parts above were toasting nicely. Hardly the fault of the heater, but for best results they should be fitted closer to the cabin sole.

Like all heaters of this type, it used a manually pressurised fuel tank to feed the paraffin to an 'Optimus'-type burner, which had to be pre-heated by burning a small quantity of methylated spirits in a moat below it.

They use no electricity at all; if there was a fan club for them, I'd join.

But burning paraffin, or any other hydrocarbon fuel for that matter, produces carbon dioxide (CO_2) and large amounts of water vapour, both of which must be vented to the atmosphere. Bulkhead-mounted heaters of this type are vented to a mushroom exhaust cap on deck, and often incorporate a short chimney to improve the upward draught. Even so, there remains a risk. Chimneys only work if the hot gas inside is sufficiently lighter than the surrounding air to create an upward draught. In cold weather the temptation is to close all ventilation hatches and portlights that face upwind. With all the remaining vents and cowls facing downwind, the main hatch open and also acting as an exhaust, the pressure within the boat can be lower than that outside, and may be sufficient to reverse the flow of fumes in the chimney. The CO_2 will then gradually replace the oxygen in the cabin, and go on to produce carbon monoxide (CO). This is highly toxic, odourless, colourless and tasteless – and if it doesn't kill you, it can leave you permanently brain damaged. The solution is to close the outlets in the ventilation system and open some of the inlets to maintain positive pressure in the cabin; then the chimney will work properly and you'll live to sail another day.

Direct Heating – Diesel Fuelled

Outwardly very similar to the paraffin types, but with some essential operational differences. Gone is the need to pressurise the fuel tank; these units are drip fed from a gravity tank, which is topped up either manually or via an electrically pumped supply from the yacht's main fuel tanks.

Admittedly there's an added degree of complexity with the latter types, but the convenience is appealing and the power consumption is insignificant; around 0.25Ah per day.

Indirect Heating

As with domestic central heating systems there are two types of systems in marine use – forced hot air (airtronic) and forced hot water (hydronic) systems. In both cases diesel is drawn from the boat's main fuel tanks and combusted in a sealed chamber located in an out-of-the-way space. Exhaust gases are vented to the atmosphere, and the burners are microprocessor-controlled, enabling automatic shutdown in the event of overheating.

Airtronic Systems

With these hot-air systems, the burner draws combustion air from outside the boat as well as from inside, and burns it in a chamber with an air-to-air heat exchanger. A blower unit then forces the heated air through flexible ducting to outlets in appropriate parts of the boat, which can be opened or closed as required. A thermostat controls the temperature, turning the system on and off automatically. But conversely, airtronic systems can be used to cool the boat. In otherwise static conditions, with the heater switched off and the blower fans operating, fresh air will be distributed through the ducting. If combined with an air-conditioning unit, cooled air can be distributed around the boat.

Hydronic Systems

The combustion parts of these systems are similar to the airtronic ones but incorporate an air-to-water heat exchanger, the cooling water from which is pumped around the boat through a system of pipes and radiators. The radiators are either convection type or, more commonly, fan-forced in much the same way as a car heater. The fan speed on each radiator can be adjusted manually, or controlled automatically by thermostats.

While more complex and expensive than their airtronic cousins, the hot water systems do provide additional benefits:

- They can be adapted to provide domestic hot water.
- They can be plumbed into the boat's engine (and generator) cooling water systems via a heat exchanger. Then, when under way and using the waste heat that would otherwise be lost, heater fuel consumption will be reduced. This also works in reverse, to preheat the engine and assist starting in cold climates.

Depending on size and the temperature setting both types can be impressively extravagant with electrical power.

PREPARING FOR THE TROPICS

At some stage in a yachtsman's life, probably when holed-up in harbour on a wet and windy bank holiday weekend, his thoughts may wander to more enticing surroundings. These musings normally take him south – France, Spain, Portugal, Cape St Vincent. Then what? Left or right? Mediterranean or Caribbean? In whichever direction his thoughts take him, wall to wall sunshine will feature strongly. But it's dodgy stuff, sunshine, and demands our respect. It's made up of three major components:

- Visible light
- Infrared radiation, which we detect as heat
- Ultraviolet light, which produces vitamin D in the human body – but over exposure to it can cause skin damage, including cancer.

By the time the sun's rays have reached the earth's surface they have been partially absorbed and weakened by various constituents of the atmosphere and deflected by air molecules, dust particles and pollution. When the sun is high overhead its rays pass through the intervening atmosphere almost vertically. In these circumstances the light is more intense, having encountered less dust and fewer air molecules than it would if the sun were low on the horizon and its rays had followed a longer, oblique passage. Towards the equator the sun progressively spends more time high overhead, cloud cover and air pollution are generally reduced, and thus in tropical regions our exposure to ultraviolet light is significantly increased.

When setting off for a long voyage, provisioning is an important part of your preparations

You need a bimini.

Keeping your Cool

Pronounced with the emphasis on the first syllable, biminis – unlike bikinis, another fair-weather image with which they may well be associated – prevent the cockpit occupants from getting too crispy when under way.

In its simplest form a bimini is merely a canvas canopy supported by a folding tubular stainless steel frame, with the whole shebang held in place by adjustable webbing straps fore and aft. When the boat is heeling, and the sun's on the windward side, sidescreen extensions hooked to the guard rails will return shade to the cockpit.

A fixed version can be designed to incorporate a boom gallows, support solar panels and provide extra handholds in the cockpit. But, unless the cover is easily removable, it's also there when you don't want it, such as in strong winds and heavy weather.

A large bimini which gives shade to the whole cockpit. But could it be removed quickly in a squall?

A smaller bimini which can quickly be folded back to the transom

On larger yachts a bimini can become quite a substantial structure, such that it would be a handful for the crew to lower it at sea. This problem is overcome by making one section of the frame fixed, usually the aft section, so that the remaining frames can fold back to it.

Ideally the frame should be fabricated in 25mm stainless steel with stainless steel fittings throughout. Aluminium tubing can be used and is cheaper in the short term, but it's hardly strong enough, will corrode, and any stainless steel fittings used with it will seize solid after a time. The canopy is best made from UV-resistant polyester or acrylic canvas, sewn up with UV-resistant thread.

Incidentally, if you've been thinking about replacing the masthead 'Windex' with an electronic wind instrument, a bimini restricting vision aloft will probably be the deciding factor.

Deck Awnings

These can be elaborate, custom-made affairs that cover the entire deck, or simple boom tents. Clearly the full-length version will keep the boat coolest, but it's worth remembering that it may need to come down in a hurry, so many will opt for the simplicity of the boom tent.

In its most basic form, it's nothing more complicated than a rectangle of fabric, eyeleted along its edges, slung over the boom and tied off to the guard rails.

Slightly more sophisticated versions incorporate lateral battens to provide additional space below. A stern gantry makes it fairly easy to fashion a particularly slick model without using battens.

If a mainsail stack-pack system with lazyjacks makes an over-the-boom version impractical, one solution is to sling it under the boom and support it with Velcro-fastened straps around the boom; another is to fit a sail track to each side of the boom and slide the awning into it. This latter approach has much to recommend it as the awning is split into two more manageable halves.

A full deck awning will help keep you cool

A foredeck awning allows you to keep the hatches open when it rains

Sewing Machines

Lightweight awnings and wind scoops can be made up by hand, but it's a whole lot easier if you have a sewing machine aboard and know how to use it. The main requirements for a marine sewing machine are:

- High level of robustness
- Stainless steel construction
- Operable by hand or electricity
- Walking foot
- Zig-zag stitch capability
- High foot lift

We managed to obtain a second-hand Reeds Sailmaker at a very reasonable price which has all of these features, and has served us admirably for a number of years.

A sewing machine is a handy thing to have on the boat

Wind Scoops

Along with windvane self-steering gears and non-skid table mats, wind scoops will always find a berth on my boat. They're fitted over a convenient deck hatch, normally made in rip-stop nylon, and supported by the inner forestay if you have one or a halyard and the jib sheets if you don't. At anchor in hot, humid conditions a wind scoop will transform conditions below – unless there's no wind to be scooped.

In non-tidal waters, an anchored boat will lay to the wind, so a forward-facing wind scoop positioned over the fore hatch will pull a cooling breeze right through the boat.

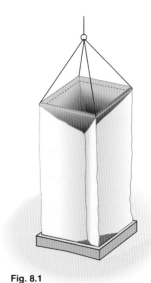

Fig. 8.1

An omni-directional wind scoop will collect wind from any angle

This wind scoop over the forehatch directs a cooling breeze below

Mary, a dab hand with a sewing machine, made ours from a single piece of spinnaker cloth. We can't claim credit for the design, but it does work very well indeed. With a forehatch hinged at the forward edge as ours is, the hatch can be left open up to around 30° in rain showers. The droplets hit the fabric, run down it and drain away on deck. Very little rain, if any, is carried below.

Alacazam has an opening portlight in the transom which helps ventilate our aft cabin. At times when it's particularly hot and humid we find a little more air wouldn't go amiss, so Mary made up a bespoke little number (see picture above) for the portlight which turns the air through 90° and wafts it breezily below. It looks a bit strange, but it works.

Tied up alongside, the wind can come from anywhere, so you will either need to position a standard wind scoop into the wind, or use a multi-directional version that picks up the breeze from any direction. The one illustrated in fig. 8.1 is a four-chambered design. As the wind shifts, the active chamber will close and the adjacent one open, providing a through-flow of air whatever the wind direction.

But wind scoops don't just scoop up wind; particularly at dusk, all kinds of flying bugs and insects will cruise in gratefully from their shoreside habitat.

A wind scoop over the stern can pull air in through a transom window

Insect Screens

Many insects are quite harmless – moths, in particular will be drawn to the cockpit light, and stunningly beautiful many of them are too. There's nothing remotely attractive about mosquitoes though. These are your enemy, and should be repelled or destroyed without mercy. The many diseases spread by mosquitoes – malaria, yellow fever, dengue fever, encephalitis and filariasis – are not caused by the insects themselves, but by micro-organisms such as bacteria, viruses and protozoans passed on when they feed on the blood of other humans and animals. Of course, a mosquito bite doesn't guarantee that you'll immediately go down with one of these exotic diseases, but it's a very good idea to keep them out of the boat if at all possible.

Our attempts to do so have only ever been partially successful – usually after having put up all the insect screens on the hatches, ports and vents do you hear the characteristic whine of a mosquito in Stuka mode, which now can't get out even if it wanted to. Time for the repellant sprays, a thorough squirting of which will leave the boat temporarily uninhabitable, at least for the crew who will now have to take their chances in the cockpit. In the West Indies there's a bug known locally as a 'no-see-um'. If their bite didn't itch like hell, you wouldn't know they existed at all.

Some manufacturers of portlights and hatches – Lewmar for one – supply removable plastic mesh insect screens which fit neatly into their products. All insect screens will reduce airflow considerably, so it's best to remove them when they're not required.

Weighted nets placed over open hatches are effective, as are wooden-framed screens fitted below, and both of these can be used in combination with a wind scoop.

A little more ingenuity is required for the main companionway. One approach is to make up a set of plywood washboards with the centres removed and replaced with mesh or netting. We've made up a canvas-framed affair held in place by wooden battens, as it's easier to stow than another set of washboards.

Taking a Dip

Unsurprisingly perhaps, you're far more likely to take a dip in the tropics than you are in the North Sea. In fact, you'll probably do lots of it and, when you come back aboard you'll need to rinse off in fresh water before going below. Salt is hydroscopic and, if allowed to get into the interior of your boat, will draw in moisture, making everything permanently damp.

At anchor in tropical climes there's no compelling reason, other than modesty perhaps, to use a shower below – a cockpit shower, either a plumbed-in unit or a solar shower bag, makes a deal of sense. I installed ours at the after end of the cockpit, so it could be used on the bathing platform – the best possible place, unless you feel a compelling need to use it in the cockpit and get all the cushions wet. Either way the presence of salt-impregnated clothing and/or bodies below decks is actively discouraged on *Alacazam*, in deference to the hydroscopic nature of salt and the absorbent qualities of upholstery.

9

ELECTRONICS

When I first ventured offshore, navigation was something of a black art involving sextants, radio direction finding (RDF) equipment, position lines and cocked hats. Now, my RDF set is probably in a museum somewhere and the sextant hasn't been out of its box in a number of years. It's still on board though, together with a Walker towed log – just in case. Cockpit instruments were independent units; the log measured speed and distance run, the depth sounder told you how much water was under your hull, and the wind instrument replicated a plan view of the masthead weathercock – "if you don't know how hard it's blowing sonny, you shouldn't be out there" – and that, together with a magnetic compass, was just about it. How things have changed.

The Global Positioning System (GPS)

While I still maintain a lingering interest in heavenly bodies, modern navigation is no longer an art – it's all done by electronic wizardry, and at its heart is GPS. This is a system of 24 satellites spread out in geo-stationary orbit some 20,000km above the earth. As the earth rotates below, at least four of the satellites are above the horizon at any one time and 'visible' from anywhere on earth. Each satellite knows precisely where it is, and kindly broadcasts this information at very accurately predetermined times. The active antenna of our GPS set records the times taken for the transmissions to reach it and computes a three-dimensional fix in terms of latitude, longitude and altitude, accurate to within a few metres.

Currently there's only one GPS system in place and it's owned and operated by the US military, who could presumably choose to block or degrade its signal to the general public. But although they've been heavily involved in various scrapes around the world in recent years, they haven't yet done so, which is a good sign. The European Community is currently building its own completely independent satellite-navigation system. Scheduled to be operational by the end of 2013, 'Galileo', as it's known, will be an orbiting system of 30 satellites giving even greater accuracy and dependability than GPS.

There's a lot more functionality to satellite navigation than position fixing. Providing you give it a clue as to your intended route (by entering a start and a destination waypoint, along with as many intermediate waypoints as may be required) it can perform a number of other useful tricks, including displays of:

- Course Made Good (CMG): the bearing from the starting point to the current position
- Cross Track Error (XTE): the distance off either side of the desired course, often shown on a 'rolling road' graphic
- Estimated Time of Arrival (ETA): the date and time of arrival at the destination based on current speed over the ground
- Estimated Time on Route: the time to go to arrival at the destination based on current speed over the ground
- Ground Speed: the velocity in knots relative to the sea bed
- Velocity Made Good (VMG): the closing speed towards the destination

Should you so wish, alarms can be set to activate when various events occur, including:

- When your anchor drags. This one will really get you out of your bunk in a hurry
- When the Cross Track Error exceeds a preset distance
- When you're within a preset distance of your destination
- When you're within a preset distance of an identified hazard, i.e. a rock, shoal or reef
- If the GPS loses its fix

All modern sets have a dedicated Man Overboard (MoB) button. Pressing this will record the current position (as a waypoint) and displays the course and distance to get back to the point at which the MoB button was activated.

Chart Plotters

Chart plotters – essentially a marriage of electronic charts and GPS – are either in the form of a software package installed on a laptop computer, or a dedicated instrument. Each has its merits, and both rely on an interface with a GPS signal. The screen is normally larger on a laptop, but some will argue that its vulnerability as a portable device makes it less attractive than a dedicated plotter, most of which are marinised and fully weatherproof.

I failed to get excited by chart plotters for a long time, preferring charts that filled the surface of my chart table to one which only filled a small screen – if I'd thought about it a little longer, perhaps I'd have realised they weren't mutually exclusive. However, while reviewing the options for a new radar at a boat show, I was persuaded to play around with a combined radar and chart plotter on a manufacturer's stand. Not only was it possible to switch between the radar display and the chart plotter display, but you could also view them simultaneously in 'split-screen' mode.

But what did it for me was the overlay mode. This enabled the radar display to overlay the chart display, with zooming in and out making it much easier to interpret when close to shore. I didn't stand a chance – it had to be mine. Installed at the chart table and fully integrated with wind, log and depth instruments it's become a very useful aid to both navigation and passage planning aboard *Alacazam* – and supplements, not replaces, my paper charts.

A chart plotter conveniently placed over the chart table

With my intended route shown on screen, and *Alacazam's* position marked by an icon, a deal of valuable information is shown graphically. For instance:

- The true (or relative) wind strength and direction is shown as a vector arrow at the icon and, similarly another arrow shows the combined effect of set and drift.
- A projected course line shows where we'll be going if all else remains constant.
- A track line shows where we've been. If this is parallel to the desired course and not to windward of it, we're doing okay. If it's diverging from the desired course and we can't sail any closer to the wind, then we'll need to tack at some stage, and it's often clear to see when this will best be done.

A typical integrated system for offshore cruising is shown in fig 117/1, the primary components being:

- Depth instrument, receiving its input from a transducer
- Speed instrument, receiving its input from a thru-hull paddlewheel log unit
- Wind instrument, receiving its input from a masthead anemometer
- Chart plotter (or GPS)
- Heading sensor, essentially a gyro-controlled fluxgate compass which may or not have a display unit
- Radar
- Autopilot

The magnetic compass remains an independent cockpit instrument, having been made redundant in the integrated system by data provided by the heading sensor.

Chartplotter

Autopilot →

← Central processor

12V

Fig. 9.1

Features of an Integrated System

While each of the instruments in an integrated system can function individually, it's only when they conspire together that additional functionality can be properly gained. For instance:

- The wind instrument can 'talk' to the speed unit and 'velocity made good to windward' can be displayed.
- True (rather than apparent) wind speed and angle off the bow can be displayed.
- With further data from the heading sensor, the heading on the opposite tack can be computed.
- The autopilot can be set to follow the route activated on the GPS or chart plotter, automatically taking account of tidal set and drift, and changing course at waypoints. Many sailors, me included, will consider this to be a step too far along the hazardous road of 'hands-free' navigation.
- The MARPA (Mini Automatic Radar Plotting Aid) collision-avoidance function is available on the radar, due to its interface with the heading sensor unit and the GPS.

All of the data available from the individual instruments can be displayed on a repeater instrument or the chart plotter.

A word of caution. A log impellor seems to hold a special fascination for small crustaceans. They just love to set up home there, and immediately set to work on slowing it down. Evicting them can only be done by removing the thru-hull unit, often a worrying process involving an impressive jet of seawater while you fumble around for the blank. The temptation is to leave them in residence, ignoring the speed-through-the-water reading from the log and relying instead on the speed-over-the-ground from the GPS. But now the chart plotter will interpret the disparity between the log reading and the GPS as an unfavourable current and display it at your boat's position accordingly. Similarly, the 'true' wind speed and direction won't be, and the displayed VMG to windward will be disappointing at best.

Radar

Fig. 9.2

Radio Detection And Ranging (RADAR) is used at sea to detect the presence of objects ('targets') at a distance, and to detect their speed if they are moving. It works by transmitting radio pulses, then detecting the echoes of these pulses from objects within the range of the pulse, and displaying them graphically as targets on the display. Being a line-of-sight device, maximum range is limited by the curvature of the earth and depends on the height of the scanner and the height of the target, as shown in fig. 9.2. Its primary function is as an aid to avoiding collision. Let's have a look at the functionality of the modern yacht radar:

- Zoom – A typical unit will have a maximum range of 24nm and will zoom down to 1/8nm. Larger, open array scanners will have a 48nm range. Short-range scales are best suited as you approach coastlines and anchorages, providing greater detail of echoes close to your boat. Long-range scales provide the best overview of your boat's position relative to land masses, large ships and squalls.
- Range Rings – Range rings are the concentric circles displayed on screen at pre-set distances, and centred at your boat's position. They're used to estimate distance between points on the display. The distance between them changes with the zoom level, typically 1/16nm at 1/8nm range and 4nm at 24nm range.
- Electronic Bearing Lines (EBLs) – This is a line drawn from your boat to the edge of the display. When rotated to align with a target it will indicate the target's relative bearing from your position.
- Variable Range Markers (VRMs) – Very much like an adjustable range ring, this will indicate the target's range. Used together with the EBL, the range and bearing of a target will be confirmed.

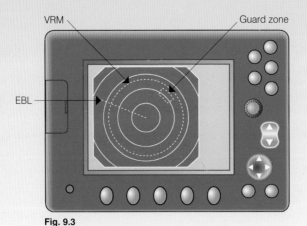

Fig. 9.3

- Guard Zones – These are areas relative to your boat's heading that can be set manually. If a target enters the zone an alarm rings. The areas set can be either a sector or a circle, as shown in fig. 9.3.
- Mini Automatic Radar Plotting Aid (MARPA) – For this collision avoidance system to be effective, accurate data of your boat's heading, speed over the ground (SOG) and course over the ground (COG) must be inputted to the radar. MARPA will track up to 10 targets and will activate an alarm if any one of them is considered to represent a collision risk.

Far offshore and away from shipping lanes, you could be forgiven for thinking that radar is largely superfluous. Not so. During the hours of darkness, the radar will see approaching rain squalls from long range, often giving you time to change course to avoid them completely or, at worst, just to suffer a glancing blow.

COMMUNICATION 10

I n Nelson's day, communicating with other vessels was done by hoisting signal flags. Samuel Morse gave us his dot-dash code in the 1830s – and it wasn't so very long ago that proud recipients of the RYA Yachtmaster Ocean certificate would have had to have a working knowledge of both methods of communication. But all that has changed.

Very High Frequency Radio (VHF)

VHF is the most popular way of communicating with other vessels and shore stations where the range allows. VHF sets are simple, compact, robust units and, compared to other two-way communication devices, inexpensive. In the UK you're required by law to have both a ship's radio licence and a VHF/DSC (Short Range) Operators Certificate.

Radio waves travel in straight lines. This means that 'if you can see it, you can talk to it'. Providing there's nothing in the way, like the curvature of the earth or a land mass to deflect it or stop it altogether, range will be between 35 to 50nm depending on the height of the antenna. On a yacht there's only one sensible place to have it; at the top of the mast. Range is also affected by power, which is measured in watts. Fixed installations can be switched between low power (1w) and high power (25w). Hand-held sets, where battery life is more critical, normally have power settings of 2.5w and 5w.

Until fairly recently, Coastguard stations worldwide and all vessels at sea were required to keep a listening watch on VHF channel 16 (156.8MHz) and 2182kHz. Vessels in distress relied on their MAYDAY call being picked up and acted upon as a result of their vigilance.

Digital Selective Calling (DSC)

From 1 January 2001, all new VHF radios had to have a built-in feature known as Digital Selective Calling, or DSC.

Prior to the advent of DSC, all VHF communication was limited to open-channel voice traffic. Everyone could eavesdrop on your conversations, and distress calls could go unanswered due to the widespread misuse of channel 16. All this changed with the arrival of DSC-equipped VHF radios. DSC uses VHF channel 70 to transmit and receive digital messages. No voice communication is permitted on that channel; it's reserved solely for DSC, which enables you selectively to contact other stations and, in digital format (an MMSI number), nominate another channel for voice communication.

In the UK, Maritime Mobile Service Identity (MMSI) numbers are assigned as a part of the ship's radio licensing procedure. These nine-digit numbers are used to identify a unique radio station. The MMSI number has a standard format and identifies the type of station, country of registration and vessel identity, and can be programmed into a DSC-equipped VHF radio just like entering a number into a mobile phone. Alternatively, groups of MMSIs can be programmed in, effectively creating a net to which communal broadcasts can be made.

But by far the most important feature of DSC is that it provides a safer way of placing a distress call to the Coastguard. A DSC distress message includes all the vital information required by the authorities – MMSI, current position and time of call – to initiate a rescue mission. Sending a distress message is as simple as selecting the nature of the distress from a scroll-down list on screen and pressing the distress button, dramatically improving the chance of a successful message than a MAYDAY call on channel 16. If the VHF set is interfaced with the GPS, then the position information is fully automated; otherwise it must be entered manually.

The Global Maritime Distress & Safety System (GMDSS)

We've got the International Convention for the Safety of Life at Sea (SOLAS) to thank for all of this. Rightly concerned with the limitations of distress calls via VHF – short range, manual alert and dependency on aural watchkeeping – SOLAS called for the development of a more efficient approach to distress situations using modern technology and automation. The new system – the Global Maritime Distress & Safety System (GMDSS) – involves geostationary satellites (INMARSAT), Coastguard shore stations and rescue co-ordination stations and it is this system that swings into action when the distress button is pressed on your DSC-enabled VHF radio.

As a result of the implementation of GMDSS the 2182kHz listening watch aboard SOLAS ships ended on 1 February 1999 and the VHF channel 16 watch ended on 1 February 2005, since when the Coastguard no longer has had a dedicated headset watch.

GMDSS incorporates a number of sub-systems, of which DSC is just one. Others include satellite communication, the Maritime Safety Information (MSI) system, the Electronic Position Indicating Radio Beacon (EPIRB) system and the Search & Rescue Transponder (SART) system.

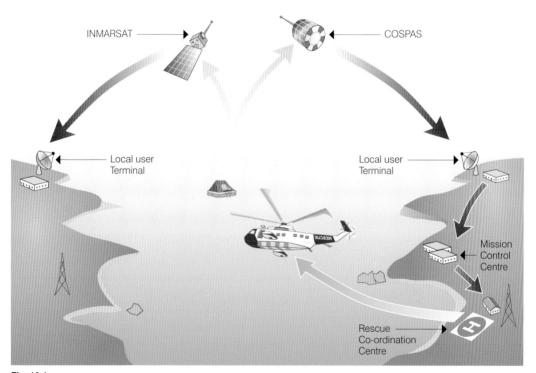

Fig. 10.1

Satellite Communication

INMARSAT, the fully commercial non-government satellite network supporting GMDSS, also provides a communication system accessible by dedicated mobile handsets (satphones). INMARSAT, founded in 1979, is the oldest satellite phone operator but other networks are now in place and operating. Of these, GLOBALSTAR and IRIDIUM are those most used by yachtsmen.

Satphones, once the size and weight of a building block, are now much like mobile phones, but rather more expensive. Outgoing calls from satellite phones to landlines and mobile phones are reasonably inexpensive, currently from around $0.15 to $2 per minute. Calls made from landlines and mobiles to satellite phones are very expensive for the caller – around $3 to $14 per minute – but free for the receiver. Making calls between different satellite phone networks is also notoriously expensive with calling rates of up to $15 per minute.

The Maritime Safety Information (MSI) System

This system provides navigational and meteorological information, plus other urgent safety-related information such as electronic chart correction data. MSI is broadcast through two independent systems – Medium Frequency telex (NAVTEX) for local MSI and by satellite or High Frequency telex (SafetyNET) for long-range MSI.

The NAVTEX installation aboard yachts normally comprises a receiver with a built-in printer and an external antenna, although there are a number of paperless units available which display the information on a scroll-down screen. Typical range is up to 400nm. Two frequencies are used – 518kHz (international frequency) and 490kHz (national frequency) – and being a line of sight system, NAVTEX may be difficult to receive when there's an obstruction between the transmitter and your antenna.

NAVTEX transmissions are sent in the English language from local stations situated worldwide. The power of each transmission is regulated so as to avoid the possibility of interference between transmitters. NAVTEX receivers can be programmed to receive specific messages and reject others – ice reports for example being unlikely to feature strongly in the Caribbean. But navigational and meteorological warnings, and search and rescue information are non-rejectable to ensure that vessels equipped with NAVTEX always receive the most vital information.

The Electronic Position Indicating Radio Beacon (EPIRB) System

We were having a spot of lunch in a yacht club with some pals who had taken a break from fitting out their Rival 38 for an Atlantic crossing. One of their recent purchases, they told us, was an EPIRB. We had to speak very loudly to make ourselves heard over the noise of a helicopter hovering nearby. We thought nothing of it at the time – after all this was Poole, home of the Royal Marines, who were always charging around in helicopters and fast landing craft. Later that day our pals had a visit from the Coastguard – what, exactly, was the nature of their distress? The EPIRB – an old 121.5MHz type – was still in one of the holdalls they had unpacked from their car and heaved aboard, and had activated as a result of the rough treatment. The Coastguard firmly but courteously explained that they could find themselves on the wrong end of a large fine, and confiscated the EPIRB. Luckily, they had upgraded to the latest type.

EPIRBs, as was so patently brought home to our pals, are used to alert search and rescue services in the event of an emergency. They do this today by transmitting a coded message on the 406MHz distress frequency, which is relayed via satellite and earth station to the nearest rescue co-ordination centre.

They work with the COSPAS-SARSAT polar orbiting satellite network, which provides true global coverage, and can determine the casualty's position by triangulation to within 3nm – or just a few metres if fitted with a built-in GPS. Most units also have a secondary distress transmitter, which operates on the old 121.5MHz and is used for homing purposes.

When an EPIRB is first purchased it must be registered with HM Coastguard, who will create a unique 15-digit hexadecimal beacon identification code – the HEX ID – which records:

- Phone numbers to call in the event of an emergency, i.e. next of kin
- A description of the vessel
- The home port of the vessel
- Any additional information that may be useful to search & rescue agencies

The distress message transmitted by the EPIRB contains information such as:

- Which country the beacon is from
- The HEX ID
- The encoded identification of the vessel in distress
- When fitted with a built-in GPS, the casualty's latitude and longitude
- Whether or not the beacon contains a 121.5MHz 'homer'

EPIRBs are radio transmitters, and as such must be included on your radio licence.

Search & Rescue Transponder (SART) System

A SART, normally present on ships rather than cruising yachts, is a portable radar transponder intended for deployment from a liferaft. It will transmit a homing signal which shows up on the radar displays of ships and aircraft involved in a search & rescue mission as a series of 12 dots, indicating the required course setting to the casualty.

Automatic Identification System (AIS)

"Westbound motor vessel two miles south of St Catherine's Point, this is the eastbound sailing yacht 'Apprehensive' one mile off your bow. Over."

Absolutely nothing. Annoying, isn't it? Did he hear us? Does he know we mean him? Are they all asleep?

In this situation, an AIS receiver would probably have got a response. So what is AIS?

AIS is a new aid to navigation operating on two dedicated VHF channels. SOLAS require that it's fitted on all ships of 300 tonnes and over when on international voyages.

These vessels are fitted with a Class A transponder which sends and receives small packages of data including vessel name, call sign, position, speed, heading, rate of turn, MMSI number, length, beam, draught and type of vessel.

Now this is the really good bit. If you've got a chart plotter and an AIS receiver (much cheaper than a transponder), and can hook it up to your VHF by an aerial splitter, the vessel's position will be indicated on your plotter. An arrow will show the direction of travel (the longer the arrow the faster the ship) and a bar on the arrow shows if the vessel is turning and which way. Hover over the ship's position with the cursor and all the vessel-related data will come up. I can remember a number of English Channel crossings when I would have paid handsomely for one of these. You're immediately aware of all ships' movements around you, course changes are shown immediately – much faster than radar. No need to call "Westbound vessel two miles south of St Catherine's Point..." etc now. You've got his name, call sign, MMSI number, the lot. Some DSC VHF radios, notably the ICOM IC-M603 and IC-M505 units, can now be purchased with an integrated AIS receiver built in.

If you want other vessels to know you're out there, you can fit a Class B transponder. These are a lot cheaper than a Class A unit but make AIS-equipped ships aware of your position, course and speed and the fact that you're a sailing vessel. Class B units do give you the option of reverting to receive mode only as, sadly, in some piratical parts of the world, invisibility and anonymity may be the wiser course of action.

Single Sideband Radio (SSB)

SSB is the sailor's favourite method of long-range communication. Once you've got the equipment installed – sadly not an inconsequential investment – all calls are free. Medium Frequency (MF) SSB has a range of around 400nm, but High Frequency (HF) will reach out for several thousand. Clearly the power required to achieve this range is considerably more than for VHF. SSB sets typically draw a peak current of around 25A when transmitting.

The component parts of an SSB installation are:

- **An MF/HF SSB transceiver** – Some SSB radios can transmit and receive on all of the HAM radio frequencies as well as the marine channels. If you have, or intend getting, a HAM radio licence then the additional cost of one of these sets may well represent excellent value for money.

- **An antenna** – Most sailboats use an insulated section of the backstay as an antenna, although some twin-masted vessels use the triatic stay if they have one. Alternatively, a fibreglass whip antenna can be used – and most usually is on catamarans that have no backstays. But whatever antenna set-up is used, without a good ground plane, radio signal and reception will be dismal.
- **A ground plane** – Bronze thru-hulls, bonded together with copper strapping, can be used successfully to form a ground plane, but this method may promote electrolysis problems. An easier approach, avoiding any electrolysis issues, is to use a sintered bronze grounding shoe to the outside of the hull, below the waterline. Of course, the best ground plane of all is provided by a steel hull.
- **An automatic antenna tuner** – SSBs transmit on a wide range of frequencies, which affects the impedance of the fixed-length antenna, which in turn affects the performance of the transmitter. An automatic antenna tuner, sometimes referred to as a coupler, matches the antenna to the output from the SSB. Manual tuners are available, and are cheaper too, but require constant readjustment with frequency changes, making the radio much more difficult to operate as a result.

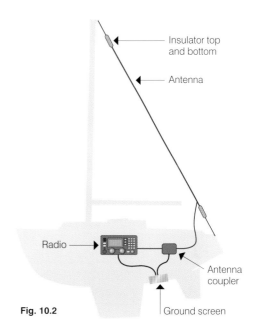

Insulator top and bottom

Antenna

Radio

Antenna coupler

Fig. 10.2

Ground screen

Top of the range SSB sets have DSC functionality built in, but if you want to use it together with the capability of being able to transmit on all marine MF/HF/VHF frequencies from a yacht then you need a GMDSS Long Range Certificate.

Such an SSB set, interfaced with a GPS (for DSC capability) and a laptop computer, provides further functionality – access to weather fax, and e-mail communication.

Weatherfax

There are around ninety weather stations around the world which regularly broadcast meteorological maps on HF SSB frequencies. With one of the weatherfax software programmes – Mscan Meteo or ICS Weather Fax6 for example – loaded into your computer, a weather map specific to your area of interest can be downloaded, often together with an associated forecast. It can then be viewed on screen, or sent to a printer if you have one, for detailed analysis.

E-mail

Just one more electronic gizmo – a radio modem – to install and then, once you've enlisted with an SSB e-mail service provider, you can send and receive e-mails wherever you are.

Most SSB e-mail service providers charge an annual subscription, so there are no line-time or by-the-bit (minutes used) charges as with mobile phone or satellite systems. There are limits on usage though.

For example, subscribers to www.sailmail.com, one of the most popular SSB ESPs, are required to limit their use of the SailMail stations to a running average of 90 minutes per week. File attachments can't be sent with outgoing emails and only certain attachments – such as weather data in .grib file format – can be received. Licensed HAM radio operators can sign-up to the Winlink 2000 system, which is completely free to use but, unlike SailMail, does not allow business transactions to be carried out over their network.

But perhaps you don't have an SSB radio and have no intention of getting one. However, you still want to send and receive e-mails from anywhere in the world. What then? You need Skymate.

Skymate

The components of this system are a small transceiver, a whip aerial and a connection to your own computer running Skymate software – and that's it! It uses the ORBCOMM satellite network, which consists of 30 satellites in low earth orbit (800km) constantly criss-crossing the globe. One of these satellites picks up your transmission and re-transmits it to one of 12 Gateway Earth Stations (GES). From the GES, the data is routed to the Gateway Control Centre (GCC), which performs message switching and system monitoring before passing the message on for final delivery by internet.

Like all satellite systems, it's not free. There's a one-time activation fee of around US$100 plus a scale of monthly charges.

Skymate is very economical with DC power, using only 60mA on standby and 2.5Ah during transmission.

Wifi Communication by Computer

Providing your laptop isn't so old that it doesn't have a wireless card built in, you may be able to hook up to a shoreside wifi network. Sometimes you can find a free one, or ride on the back of someone's unsecured home network, but more often than not you'll have to pay for it. If you see a cluster of cruising yachts anchored close inshore near a building, you can probably safely assume there's free wifi.

With the standard built-in set-up in most laptops, wifi performance can be more than a tad disappointing, but it can be considerably improved by installing a signal enhancer. A unidirectional type will be fine when you're tied up alongside and know where the wifi transmitter is. Just plug in the unit to a USB port on your laptop, point it at the transmitter and you're in business. At anchor, with the yacht swinging around with wind and tide, you'll find the unidirectional type will be unreliable.

In this situation an externally mounted omni-directional type is far superior. These take the form of an active antenna around a metre long which is mounted (either permanently fixed, or hoisted on a halyard) as far above deck as is practicable.

When connected, you should be able to e-mail all those attachments that you couldn't with SSB e-mail – and you can now surf the internet.

A unidirectional wifi signal enhancer hooked into a USB port

If you power your laptop through an inverter, it should be a pure sinewave type, or the performance of your computer may be compromised. But as most laptops operate at around 19v DC it does seem strange to invert 12v DC to 220v (or 110v) AC and then via its own AC adapter to 19v DC. I get around all this by using a Targus power adapter, one end of which plugs into the 12v socket and the other to the power socket on the laptop. An added bonus is that I no longer need an expensive pure sinewave inverter – a much cheaper modified sinewave model being fine for charging power tools and running the sewing machine.

Broadband Dongle

Just the thing if wifi isn't available. A broadband dongle is a USB device that you plug into your computer to provide mobile access to the internet. The dongle contains a SIM card that gives you access to the 3G network that currently covers almost all of the UK and many other countries worldwide. Most of the major mobile phone companies provide them, the monthly fee normally giving you up to 3Gb of data transfer. But, before using one of these outside of the UK you'll need to check if the service provider has coverage in the areas you intend to cruise – and how much it will cost.

An internet connection via a mobile 'dongle'

If you hadn't done so beforehand, it's worth downloading the free software from www.skype.com and investing in a microphone headset, or a USB phone.

Skype

Skype is a program for telephone communication via the internet. At best, call charges are free, as when talking to another person also on Skype. At worst, for example when calling a mobile or landline number, they're inexpensive.

Providing the person you wish to talk to has downloaded Skype to his computer and you're both on-line, you can talk free for as long as you like. It makes no difference if he's in the house next door or on a yacht the other side of the world.

You can also use Skype to contact someone on a mobile phone or landline, but for this there's a small charge – typically less than £1 for an hour-long international call.

11

FRIDGES, FREEZERS & COOKERS

Even in a well-designed galley, there's no doubt that cooking at sea can be a perilous affair. Where else but on a yacht would you even contemplate handling boiling liquids and hot metal utensils on a rolling, lurching platform? A well-designed and constructed cooker will go a long way towards protecting you from these very real risks.

Cookers

What goes to make a good cooker for an offshore yacht? Safety, practicality and durability are the essential ingredients, and in particular:

- **Flame failure devices (on gas cookers)** – These are thermocouples which will only allow gas to flow to the burner if a minimum temperature is maintained. They come into play when the flame goes out, maybe as the result of a gust of wind blowing down the companionway, or a liquid boiling over. Within seconds, the burner cools and the gas is shut off. Without them, gas would continue to flow and, being heavier than air, would accumulate in the bilge where the smallest spark – maybe even from static electricity – could ignite it and cause total destruction of the boat and its occupants. Flame failure devices on all burners are essential – this is no area to look for cost savings. A cooker that doesn't have them has no place on a boat.

- **Gimballing** – This must be adequate for all angles of heel on both tacks. This is largely dependent on where the cooker is located in the galley. On some boats the cooker has almost unlimited swing on one tack but collides with the outboard face of its recess on the other. If the crash bar in front of the cooker is too close to it, the inboard swing can trap unwary fingers. I know; ours was; it did, twice, until I moved it. The final length of the supply hose to gas cookers should be flexible armoured hose to protect it from chafing or pinching when the cooker swings, and it should be possible to lock the gimbals to prevent the cooker from swinging unexpectedly when alongside.

Stove installations should have a safety bar and a waist strap

- **Fiddles and pan clamps** – A sturdy fiddle rail should be permanently fitted in place, together with removable pan clamps for each of the top burners.

- **Secure grill** – The grill pan must be retained in place under its burners by a lip or some other device, or your tomatoes, sausages and bacon will quickly find themselves on the galley sole. They're never quite the same after that.

- **Lockable oven door** – I once witnessed a fully loaded casserole dish launch itself across the galley, with predictably messy results, when the oven door burst open on a particularly violent roll. A lockable oven door will prevent this happening.

- **Construction** – Solid, corrosion-proof construction, preferably all stainless steel. The cooker should be manufactured with cleaning, maintenance and servicing in mind, and be capable of being taken apart and reassembled with little more than a screwdriver.

We've mentioned gas cookers and while there's no doubt that LPG in either butane or propane form is the most popular fuel, were it not for its explosive nature, the case for it would be overwhelming.

While other fuels like paraffin (kerosene) are sometimes difficult to come by, and the much less efficient methylated spirits (alcohol) are inherently safer, a properly designed and installed LPG system will mitigate the safety issues to acceptable levels. Such a system will incorporate the following features:

- A dedicated gas bottle locker, ventilated to the atmosphere, draining overboard and sealed from the rest of the vessel. The gas bottles will be firmly secured within it.

- The regulator will be mounted on the bulkhead within the locker, rather than screwed directly into the bottle. A pair of bottles can then be connected to it via a double manifold and high-pressure hose, enabling easy changeover from one bottle to the other.

- A remotely operated 12v solenoid switch to turn the gas supply off when considered prudent.

- A bubbler-type leak detector to check daily the gas integrity of the installation.

- A simple manual turn-off tap close to the cooker.

Fig.11.1

Gas cookers should ideally be capable of running on either butane or propane. However, there is a case for a propane set-up for long-distance cruisers due to its availability worldwide and its willingness, unlike butane, to operate in freezing conditions.

And while, in freezing conditions, the heat generated below by a cooker on full song will be appreciated by the crew, it will not be so in the tropics, where 'sweating over a hot stove' becomes more than just a cliché.

If you can't Stand the Heat...

Get a barbecue.

I've already stated my ineptitude in the cooking department. But I have to qualify that statement – except on the barbie; now that is my domain. People come for miles…

A stainless steel marine barbie, firmly secured to the taff rail, is a great asset. Two types are available:

First catch the fish then cook them on the barbie!

- Conventionally fuelled by charcoal or
- by LPG (plumbed in or by a screw-on bottle)

I'm told that the LPG ones eventually corrode at the terminal fitting, and end up being fuelled by charcoal. Ours is a charcoal-burning Magna unit, which provides sterling service. Charcoal's available pretty much everywhere but, where it isn't, dried coconut husks will probably be around and they will do nicely. Vegetarians excepted, if you haven't tasted really freshly caught fish, grilled lightly on the barbie, then you haven't lived. And while the coals are still glowing, throw on a few bananas in their skins and leave them until they're totally black.

Refrigeration

Robert Boyle started it all in 1662, when he recognised the inversely proportional relationship between the absolute pressure and volume of a gas, when the temperature is kept constant within a closed system. Later work by other thermodynamic luminaries resulted in the Combined Gas Law, which states that:

$$\frac{PV}{T} = k, \text{ where P is pressure, V is volume, T is temperature and k is a constant.}$$

This means that if you mess around with the pressure and volume of a gas, its temperature will change – and that explains a lot of what goes on inside a fridge. The rest is down to the particular properties of the refrigerant gas, one of which is that it liquefies at a temperature of -15.9°C.

The component parts of a fridge are a compressor, a condenser, an expansion valve and a cold plate.

They work together to produce the following cycle of events:

- The compressor compresses the refrigerant gas, reducing its volume and thereby raises its temperature, and pumps it along to the condenser.
- The condenser allows the refrigerant to dissipate the heat arising from the change in pressure.
- As it cools, the refrigerant condenses into liquid form and flows through the expansion valve.
- Here, the liquid refrigerant flows from a high-pressure zone to a low-pressure zone, causing it to expand, vaporise and cool rapidly as it enters the cold plate.
- The coils inside the cold plate allow the refrigerant to absorb heat from the surrounding air, which is of course the inside of the fridge.
- The heat-bearing gas returns to the compressor and the cycle is repeated, further lowering the temperature of the fridge.
- When the temperature has dropped to the temperature set on the thermostat, the power to the compressor is turned off until such time as it has fallen to the 'start-up' temperature.

The system performance depends on the characteristics of the individual components, some of which are more suited for certain applications than others.

The Compressor

These are either powered by the yacht's electrical system or driven by a belt from the main engine.

Electrically powered compressors are normally of the diaphragm type, although very large units may be of a piston design. This latter type, resembling a reciprocating engine, is more costly to manufacture but can be stripped and serviced by a competent mechanic, whereas the diaphragm type is almost invariably a sealed unit which must be replaced when it fails. Nearly all proprietary 'packaged units' incorporate a diaphragm compressor due to their compactness, efficiency and quiet operation.

Piston or diaphragm, both types have a healthy appetite for electricity.

Engine-driven versions, developed from car air-conditioning units, are engaged through an electromagnetic clutch, either automatically or simply by throwing a switch. They're very powerful and of course make no demand (other than a few milliamps for the thermostat) on the boat's electrical system. But they do depend on running the main engine – typically an hour a day in a well set-up system – which, on a sailing vessel, you may not always want to do.

The Condenser

This, a heat exchanger, will be one of two types – air cooled or seawater cooled. Air-cooled units are the simpler, more elegant solution and, if installed below the waterline where the bilge air is at a similar temperature to the sea, they can be remarkably efficient – particularly so if a steady stream of cool air is wafted over them by a small fan. But they can struggle a bit in hot climates where the difference between the ambient air temperature and that required inside the fridge may not be enough to dissipate the heat in the refrigerant gas. In these conditions, and most definitely if the cooling unit is installed in the engine room, a seawater type will be required. A circulation pump draws in cooling water from outside the boat and, water being a much better conductor of heat than air, will carry away the heat more effectively. An innovative approach by one manufacturer manages to achieve seawater cooling without an electrically driven pump. A special skin-fitting replaces the one normally fitted at the galley sink. This contains a spiral heat exchanger, through which the refrigerant gas passes, transferring its heat to the seawater. The slightest movement of the boat, even when tied-up alongside, is enough to pump away the heat. Clever stuff.

The Cold Plate

Again there are two types – the basic evaporator plate and the cold storage 'eutectic' plate.

The basic evaporator plate cools down quickly but, equally quickly, warms up again. Consequently the thermostat will be regularly kicking the compressor in and out – a 'constant cycling' system. In hot climates the compressor may be running for 45 minutes or so in every hour, so the current drain will be high.

The cold storage 'eutectic' plate differs from the basic evaporator plate in that the coils are immersed in a liquid that freezes and melts at minimum temperature – a 'eutectic' liquid. This takes a bigger effort to cool the plate down, normally done in one hit by an oversized compressor, but it then retains its 'cool' for longer, gradually dispensing through a state of being frozen solid to partially thawed out. Clearly this is the type of cold plate to use with an engine-driven compressor, and if using the Automatic Start-Up system described below.

System Management

The Automatic Start-Up (ASU) system senses when surplus electrical energy is available, either from the alternator, solar panels or wind generator. It then speeds up the compressor to freeze rapidly the eutectic liquid in the cold plate and keeps it frozen until surplus energy is no longer available, at which point it stops the compressor until either:

- The cold plate falls to a predetermined temperature, whereon the compressor restarts in a low-speed, low-current mode to maintain the temperature at that level, or
- more surplus energy becomes available, whereon it restarts the compressor in high-speed mode, freezing down the cold plate again.

Top or Front Opening?

It's often said that a top-opening fridge is more efficient than the front-opening type, because the cold doesn't 'fall out' when you take the lid off. True, but in my experience, whatever you need will be at the bottom, which means that half the stuff will have to come out before you can get at it. Hot arms will displace the cold air and the stuff you've taken out will start to warm. In a front-opening fridge, all the goodies are on shelves – easy to find and remove, so the door can quickly be closed. I've not done the experiment, but I'll bet there's not much in it. What is important is the quality and thickness of the insulation – at least 100mm of it – and the condition of the seal at the lid or door.

Freezers

We don't have one of these on *Alacazam*, and there are times when we regret it. On passage we look forward to the occasional fish that has thrown itself gratefully upon my trolled lure. But they're not always conveniently pan-sized and, unless you want to eat large portions of it morning, noon and night for about three days, a decent-sized one will have to be returned from whence it came. But not if you've got a freezer.

I've mentioned fish a couple of times in this chapter, so it might be an appropriate time to describe briefly how to catch them.

Filling the Freezer

A simple handline and a few lures will get you well on the way to putting some fresh protein and healthy Omega 3 fatty acids into your diet. All you need is about 30m of 300lb main line, a lead sinker (optional), a heavy-duty swivel to prevent twists, a 300lb mono leader and a lure. Rig it and tow it astern. It's important to include a snubber to absorb the shock-load of a striking fish, which may otherwise tear itself free. Pretty unsporting of it, but it happens.

The lure could be a skirted type intended to imitate a squid, or a plug type which wriggles around like a small fish. The skirted lures will operate close to the surface, but the plug type has a steel or plastic vane at the front end which will get it down a few feet.

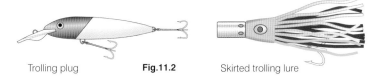

Trolling plug   **Fig.11.2**   Skirted trolling lure

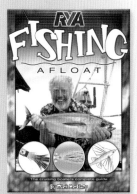

RYA code G72

Your success will see a very lively and often alarmingly toothy fish leaping around on the cockpit sole. It deserves to die quickly and painlessly.

If this subject intrigues you in any small way, you may want to take a look at 'RYA Fishing Afloat'.

12 THE HEADS

After computers, marine toilets are probably the most exasperating machines ever invented. Clearly 'GIGO' (Garbage In, Garbage Out) applies to them both – perhaps that has something to do with it. Without going into too much detail, regular use is perhaps the best medicine for them, as otherwise the seals tend to dry out and a 'no go' situation prevails.

Their malicious streak can come to a head (sorry) in a toilet installed below the waterline, where it has the capability of sinking the boat if not fitted with siphon breaks on both inlet and outlet pipes. Otherwise, for a toilet installed below the waterline, or one which becomes below the waterline when the boat is heeled, pumping flushing water in (and waste water out) will induce a siphon effect – flooding and eventually sinking your boat.

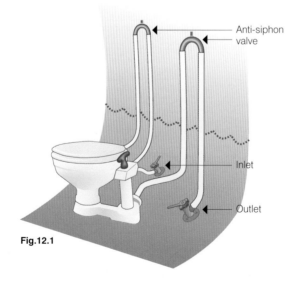

Anti-siphon valve

Inlet

Outlet

Fig.12.1

Holding Tanks

For years, we sailors (along with fish, birds and other mammals) have been polluting the oceans – and nature has easily been able to deal with it. But in recent times, recreational sailing has mushroomed and, where we have flocked together in ever-larger marinas close to towns and tourist areas, our concentrated efforts are often clearly visible.

Although there's currently no consistency at European level on the matter of sewage-holding tanks for recreational craft, some EU member states have enacted national legislation concerning those vessels equipped with a holding tank, while others are still sitting on the fence.

Before too long yet more EU legislation will befall us, and we'll all be required to install a holding tank. In the USA the requirement is already pretty much universal, and enthusiastically enforced by the waterborne 'potty police'. These gentlemen will board your boat uninvited and, if they find your holding tank diverter valve in the 'discharge' position, you'll find yourself in a spot of bother.

A typical holding tank installation is shown in fig 12.2.

This arrangement, through appropriate use of the diverter valve, will either discharge toilet waste overboard or to the holding tank for proper disposal later. Retro-fitting a rigid plastic holding tank is likely to test the ingenuity of most boat owners, who will already have claimed all suitable spaces for other useful purposes. A flexible tank may provide a solution, although if it chafes through it will provide rather more.

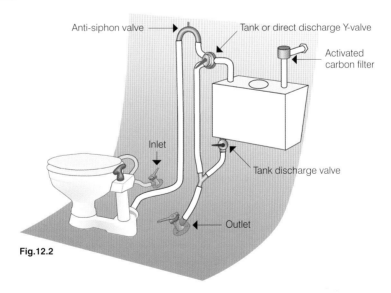

Anti-siphon valve

Tank or direct discharge Y-valve

Activated carbon filter

Inlet

Tank discharge valve

Outlet

Fig.12.2

To avoid unpleasant odours and disperse any gaseous arisings, the vent pipe should be not less than 1½″ (38mm) and exit the hull side just below the gunwale. Wherever possible it should be left permanently open to allow both the discharge of displaced air and the free flow of incoming air, thus retaining the effluent in an aerobic condition. Tanks with small breathers will almost certainly turn anaerobic. It's in this latter condition, created by the absence of oxygen, that unpleasant odours occur.

13

THE ENERGY EQUATION

Funny stuff, electricity. Invisible and weightless, yet capable of improving your life enormously if you treat it with respect – and ending it abruptly if you don't.

Modern cruising yachts demand increasing amounts of its energy to power their ever more complex systems, so adequate means of both storing and generating it are of vital importance. Fundamentally – if disappointment is to be avoided – the relationship between supply and demand must be properly managed, i.e. Energy In = Energy Out, which means you can only take out what you put in, rather like a well-managed deposit account – hence 'battery banks', possibly?

To manage our energy equation properly, we need to evaluate both sides of it:

- The 'demand' side: How much energy do we require to feed our electrical systems?
- The 'supply' side: How can we generate and store enough of it to meet that requirement?

The Electrical Requirement

To calculate our daily domestic electrical requirement we must first make a list of all electrical equipment on board, and apply a current rating to each item. If you've got a battery monitor installed in the system and it's capable of being switched to read amps, you'll be able, by turning on one item at a time, to read the actual current draw for each item – otherwise you'll have to work it out. Ratings can usually be found on equipment nameplates or in their manuals, and will be expressed in terms of power (measured in watts) or current draw (measured in amps).

The relationship between power and current is expressed as:

$$\text{Power (W)} = \text{Current (A)} \times \text{System Voltage (V)}$$

To derive amps from watts, simply transpose this equation and divide the wattage by the system voltage. For example, a 6 watt navigation light bulb in a 12 volt system will draw 0.5 amps – which, if it's switched on for 10 hours each day when under way will have consumed 5 amp/hours (Ah). Continuing in this vein for each item of equipment will produce a table much like the ones shown here.

Appliance	Current	Under way (24 hours)		At anchor (24 hours)	
		Usage (hours)	Current consumption (amp/hours)	Usage (hours)	Current consumption (amp/hours)
Anchor light	0.90A			10	9.00Ah
Anchor windlass	50.00A			0.1	5.00Ah
Autopilot	4.00A	24	96.00Ah		
Bilge pump	5.00A	0.1	0.50Ah	0.1	0.50Ah
Cabin lights (based on 3 @ .6Ah)	1.80A	1	1.80Ah	4	7.20Ah
Chart Plotter (including GPS)	0.80A	24	19.20Ah		
Chart table light	0.30A	2	0.60Ah		
Cockpit instruments	0.30A	24	7.20Ah		
Cockpit light	1.00A			4	4.00Ah
Compass light	0.20A	10	2.00Ah		
Deck lights	1.70A	0.25	0.43Ah		
Distribution panel	0.10A	24	2.40Ah	24	2.40Ah
Fresh water pump	4.00A	2	8.00Ah	2.00	8.00Ah
Fridge (say 50% cut-in)	4.00A	12	48.00Ah	12.00	48.00Ah
Gas alarm	0.60A	24	14.40Ah	24.00	14.40Ah
Laptop computer	8.00A			2.00	16.00Ah
Masthead (steaming) light	0.90A	1	0.90Ah		
Navigation lights	3.70A	1	3.70Ah		
Navtex	0.40A	24	9.60Ah	24.00	9.60Ah
Radar (standby)	1.00A	10	10.00Ah		
Radar (transmit)	2.50A	3	7.50Ah		
Shower pump	6.50A			0.25	1.63Ah
SSB (standby)	1.00A	24	24.00Ah	24.00	24.00Ah
SSB (transmit)	25.00A	0.5	12.50Ah	0.50	12.50Ah
Stereo	0.90A			2.00	1.80Ah
Tricolour	2.20A	9	19.80Ah		
Ventilation fans	1.00A			4.00	4.00Ah
VHF (Standby)	0.30A	24	7.20Ah	24.00	7.20Ah
VHF (Transmit)	1.20A	1	1.20Ah	1.00	1.20Ah
Watermaker	9.00A	1	9.00Ah	4.00	36.00Ah
Total requirement:			305.93		212.43

This calculation, though, remains an estimate. For example:

- In cold weather the fridge will draw less power than in hot weather.
- In rough weather the autopilot would use more power than when it's calm.
- Hours of darkness will vary with latitude and time of year, affecting current draw for navigation and domestic lighting.
- You'll use the watermaker more when you've got guests aboard, etc.
- There are start-up currents and other losses that have been ignored.

So it's approximate, but indicates that you'll need to replace around 310Ah each day when you're sailing and 220Ah when you're at anchor.

The under way current consumption clearly presents the worst-case scenario, but ignores the fact that more power is consumed during the night than during the day. An analysis of the table on page 113 produces the one on page 115, which indicates that the domestic battery bank will be drawn down by 175Ah during the night-time hours – an average discharge of around 14.6A over 12 hours.

Fig.13.1

Appliance	Under way			
	Day (12 hours)		Night (12 hours)	
	Usage (hours)	Current consumption (amp/hours)	Usage (hours)	Current consumption (amp/hours)
Autopilot	12.00	48.00Ah	12.00	48.00Ah
Bilge pump	0.05	0.25Ah	0.05	0.25Ah
Cabin lights (based on 3 @ .6Ah)			1.00	1.80Ah
Chart Plotter/GPS	12.00	9.60Ah	12.00	9.60Ah
Chart table light			2.00	0.60Ah
Cockpit instruments			24.00	7.20Ah
Compass light			10.00	2.00Ah
Deck lights			0.25	0.43Ah
Distribution panel & DCM	12.00	1.20Ah	12.00	1.20Ah
Fresh water pump	1.00	4.00Ah	1.00	4.00Ah
Fridge (say 50% cut-in)	6.00	24.00Ah	6.00	24.00Ah
Gas alarm	12.00	7.20Ah	12.00	7.20Ah
Masthead (steaming) light			1.00	0.90Ah
Navigation lights			1.00	3.70Ah
Navtex	12.00	4.80Ah	12.00	4.80Ah
Radar (standby)			10.00	10.00Ah
Radar (transmit)			3.00	7.50Ah
SSB (standby)	12.00	12.00Ah	12.00	12.00Ah
SSB (transmit)	0.25	6.25Ah	0.25	6.25Ah
Tricolour			9.00	19.80Ah
VHF (Standby)	12.00	3.60Ah	12.00	3.60Ah
VHF (Transmit)	0.50	0.60Ah	0.50	0.60Ah
Watermaker	1.00	9.00Ah		
Total requirement:		130.50		175.43

So what's the difference between amps (A) and amp-hours (Ah)? The best way to explain it is by example. If an appliance drawing 5A was to run for 1 hour, its consumption would amount to 5Ah. This would be the same as an appliance drawing 1A running for 5 hours – again the consumption would be 5Ah. So amp-hours are simply the (average) amperage drawn, multiplied by the time in hours. Amp-hours are also used to describe battery capacity. In this context the plot thickens.

Sizing the Domestic Battery Bank

It's important to match the battery bank capacity to the current requirement. Too low a capacity and the charge times will be long and frequent; too large and it will be difficult to charge it fully through an engine-driven alternator.

Before we go any further, we should have a look at battery amp-hour ratings. These refer to the available current over a nominal period until a specified voltage is reached. Rates are normally specified as either a 10-hour rate or, almost invariably these days, at a 20-hour rate. This

A pair of AGM batteries totalling 420Ah

means that a battery rated at 100Ah at a 10-hour rate with a final voltage per cell of 1.7 volts is capable of delivering 10 amps for 10 hours, when a cell voltage of 1.7 volts is attained. Thus a 6-cell 12 volt battery at this stage would show a residual voltage of 10.2 volts – or flat, not a good shape for a battery to be in. Don't be fooled into thinking that a battery rated at 20 hours is 'bigger' than one rated at 10 hours for the same capacity. It isn't – it's the other way round. If you were to choose a 100Ah battery rated at 20 hours, it would have 10% to 15% less capacity than a 100Ah battery rated at 10 hours.

Battery voltages		Open Circuit Voltages
12.8v	Fully charged	An open circuit is one where the battery has been allowed to stabilise after charging and all DC loads have been turned off.
12.6v	80% charged 20% discharged	
12.4v	70% charged 30% discharged	
12.2v	50% charged 50% discharged	If voltages are measured immediately after charging, the voltages could measure 13.4v due to the presence of surface charge on the battery plates. To remove this, apply a load of 15 to 20 watts for 10 minutes.
12.0v	30% charged 70% discharged	
11.8v	15% charged 85% discharged	

So, a battery's capacity depends on how fast you discharge it. It's very important to understand that the faster you drain your batteries, the less capacity you will have at your disposal. The good news is that the converse is also the case. Discharge your batteries at a slower rate than the one specified and you will find that you have more capacity than you thought you had.

Of course we don't want to discharge our batteries until they're flat – they won't stand too many such cycles until they're ruined. Conventional wisdom has it that they should only be discharged to 50% of their capacity. So for our 12-hour current draw of 175A, would we need a battery bank of 350Ah? In an ideal world that would be correct, but the reality is rather different. With the alternators supplied as standard equipment on most yachts, batteries are rarely above 70% charged and can't be fully recharged with the standard regulator fitted, and the resulting sulphation on the battery banks will reduce capacity by a further 10%. Thus, in this example a battery bank of 2 x 175Ah batteries could only be considered as the absolute minimum, and only then if you've fitted a high-output alternator and a 'smart' regulator to minimise the losses – and are prepared to run the engine every 12 hours.

Ideally, the current draw should be matched to the discharge characteristics of the batteries. As we know, the faster a battery is discharged above its nominal rating, the lower the real amp-hour capacity will be. Conversely, the slower a battery is discharged below its nominal rating, the higher the real amp-hour capacity. In our example the latter case would appear to be true – a 14.6Ah draw down against a nominal discharge of 17.5Ah from each of the 175Ah batteries. But as the batteries are rated at 10 hours the battery will discharge longer and faster during the 12-hour period of the draw down, so it would be prudent to install two batteries of the next size up.

Power Conservation

In our example there are several things that could be done to reduce the daily consumption:

- LED (Light Emitting Diode) lights. These draw a fraction of the current taken by a standard incandescent light and have an exceptionally long service life. I reckon if the anchor light, tricolour, cockpit light and cabin lights were replaced with LEDs then at least 15 amps could be shaved off the under way consumption and a similar amount off when at anchor. A further benefit of a combined anchor/tricolour LED light is that you won't have to scoot up the mast to change a blown bulb – a prospect I view with increasing dismay these days.
- The autopilot. If you had windvane self-steering it wouldn't use any power at all, reducing the daily drawdown by a whopping 31%.
- The fresh water pump. Turn it off on passage and use the hand pumps.

Battery Types

Batteries operate on the principle that a voltage develops across two electrodes of dissimilar metals when they are immersed in an electrolyte. A 12 volt battery is made up of six individual cells connected in series within an outer plastic casing, the voltage generated in each cell being 2.1 volts.

The vast majority of batteries in boats today are of the lead-acid type. These can be divided into two general categories:

1. Flooded Cell – often known as 'liquid lead-acid'
2. Valve-Regulated Lead Acid (VRLA)

Let's look at these two types in more detail.

Liquid Lead Acid Batteries

Largely due to their relatively low cost, these are the most common. Using a dilute solution of sulphuric acid in liquid form as the electrolyte, they have positive and negative plates constructed of lead dioxide and lead respectively. This type can be divided into distinct categories:

- Starter batteries, similar to the ones we have in our cars. In these the plates are very thin to allow the rapid release of electrical energy required to crank an engine. Unfortunately, this also makes the plates susceptible to damage, particularly if the battery is deep cycled.
- Deep-cycle (or 'traction'). Here the plates are much thicker, meaning the battery can be deeply discharged without undue damage. These very robust batteries will last a long time but are unsuitable for engine starting.
- So-called 'leisure' batteries, which are a compromise between the two and a firm favourite of many boat owners.

Not being sealed, flooded batteries lose water from the electrolyte due to evaporation and will need the occasional top-up. You must always use distilled or de-ionized water for this. Don't be tempted to use tap water as it contains minerals and other impurities which may pollute and damage the cells.

The gas given off is a mixture of oxygen and hydrogen – mainly the latter – so there's always a theoretical risk of explosion if a naked flame or spark occurs. However, with both gases being lighter than air, a vented battery box will see them rapidly and harmlessly assimilated into the atmosphere. One more thing – if the electrolyte comes into contact with seawater, chlorine gas is produced, which is most definitely not what you want.

Gel Cell Batteries

Unlike a normal lead acid battery, gel cells use a thixotropic gel to immobilise the electrolyte. These VRLA batteries have some significant benefits over flooded batteries, along with some disadvantages. Let's take a look:

- They're sealed, maintenance free and the fully absorbed electrolyte won't leak if the casing is damaged.
- Under normal operating conditions there's virtually no gassing. Unlike flooded cells, they're hermetically sealed and operate under pressure to recombine the oxygen and hydrogen produced during the charge process back into water. If the pressure mounts too high, a valve releases the gases to the atmosphere.
- They can be installed anywhere and in any orientation. On their side in the bilges is fine – they will even operate safely underwater.
- While flooded cells lose up to 1% per day due to self-discharge, VRLAs lose no more than 3% per month.
- Gel cell batteries are probably the most sensitive to overcharge abuse, with a maximum voltage of 14.4 volts being recommended. It's important to match the charge regime to the battery type.
- They cost up to 50% more than equivalent lead acid batteries.

Absorbed Glass Mat (AGM) Batteries

These are the latest step in the development of sealed batteries, and they're the ones for me. Strictly speaking, these are of the liquid lead acid type but, as their name suggests, the electrolyte is held by capillary action in a fine fibrous glass mat so doesn't slosh about. As with the gel cell type, they can be mounted up anyway and won't leak if the casing is breached. Thanks to their low internal resistance, AGM batteries will accept high charging currents – meaning they can be charged very rapidly, though it's recommended that voltages be capped at 14.4 volts. This characteristic also allows them to release power quickly, making them suitable for engine starting. Smaller AGMs are made specifically for that purpose. On *Alacazam* we've installed a Redflash 750, just 169mm long x 179mm wide x 147mm high, which spins my Yanmar 30 over very nicely.

All AGMs are comparatively expensive batteries but, if treated properly, they offer many advantages and have a long service life. Because of this, they could even be more economical in the long run.

Power Generation

Production sailboats 'straight out of the box' rely solely on shore power and engine-charging to top up their batteries. Fine for the coastal sailor, but we long-distance chaps need to be more resourceful. Before we enter the fascinating world of alternative energy systems – green power – let's take a look at engine-driven alternators.

Engine Driven Alternators

Let's assume that we fitted two 200Ah lead acid deep-cycle batteries to satisfy our daily power consumption in the example above. A rule of thumb is that the alternator output current should be at around 30% of the battery bank capacity – so we need a 120A alternator. Odds are that the one supplied with your engine will be rated considerably lower, and will come with a standard car-type regulator built in. If we're going to stand any chance at all of fully charging that battery bank we need a 120A alternator and a 'smart' regulator to replace the 'daft' one. What's that all about then?

Perhaps we're being a little unkind to the car-type regulator. After all, it doesn't need sparkling capabilities to do its job. In just starting the engine, car batteries are rarely depleted below 5% of their maximum capacity, whereupon they are quickly restored to full charge by the alternator. As we've already seen, yacht batteries are often heavily discharged and need more than a quick squirt of amps to bring them back to full charge. The regulator controls alternator output by monitoring the level of charge in the battery. At 50% discharge a battery will gratefully suck in everything that is thrown at it, but as the charge level rises the regulator will sense, and have to compensate for, an electrical 'back-pressure' from the batteries, preventing the charge from penetrating the cell matrix. At a charge level of around 70% this all gets a bit much for the car-type regulator, which gives up.

What has actually happened is that charge has built up on the surfaces of the plates, resulting in an apparently high battery voltage which fools the regulator into thinking it has done its job.

Smart Regulators

At this point a cerebrally superior, multi-microchipped regulator will sense that all is not as it appears, and begin cycling the charging voltage either side of the battery gassing voltage to allow full current diffusion throughout the full depth of the battery plates. The relationship between battery input and alternator output is continually monitored while the engine is running, providing a continual restoration of battery charge.

Charging Periods

With an efficient charging system, we can now take a stab at the charging interval and periods. The following comes with a health warning, as it's an approximate calculation:

Under way, daily requirement 306 amps, battery bank 400 amp-hours

Charging interval $= ($ battery bank (Ah) x allowable draw down (50%)$/$daily requirement (A) $)$ x 24 hours

$\qquad = ($ 400 x 50%$/$306 $)$ x 24

$\qquad = 15$ hours

Charging period $= ($ battery bank (Ah) x allowable draw down (50%)$/$alternator output – hourly drawdown $)$ + charging loss

$\qquad = ($ 400 x 50%$/$120 - 12.75 $)$ x 120%

$\qquad = 2.25$ hours

These means that you'd have to run your engines twice a day for two hours to keep the batteries topped up when under way – not a joyful prospect. Let's take a look at it at anchor:

Charging interval $= ($ battery bank (Ah) x allowable draw down (50%)$/$daily requirement (A) $)$ x 24 hours

$\qquad = ($ 400 x 50%$/$212 $)$ x 24

$\qquad = 23$ hours

Charging period $= ($ battery bank (Ah) x allowable draw down (50%)$/$alternator output – hourly drawdown $)$ + charging loss

$\qquad = ($ 400 x 50%$/$120 - 8.83 $)$ x 120%

$\qquad = 2.15$ hours

At anchor then, you'd need to run your engine once a day for two hours or more – which may not impress your neighbours. But if you incorporated alternative energy systems into your charging regime, then your use of the engine would reduce dramatically. We'll get back to this a little later.

Green Power

It seems appropriate for a sailor to run his engine only when it's absolutely necessary, mainly to retain for better use the pennies that are increasingly gobbled up by the ever-rising cost of fuel. There's something very satisfying about using nature's free resources rather than her limited and messy hydrocarbon deposits to pursue our sailing endeavours. I've already waxed long and lyrical about windvane self-steering – unapologetically so – and I'm now about to do the same with wind and solar-powered generating devices.

Wind Generators

Unsurprisingly, wind generators are more effective in some areas than others. In the Mediterranean for example, where calm conditions are frequent, solar panels may be a better option. On a trade-wind Atlantic crossing with the wind astern, their performance will probably be disappointing owing to the reduced relative wind speed. Having arrived in the West Indies it will be a different matter, where beam winds and breezy anchorages will give good 24-hour charging.

The power is generated by spinning a DC generator or an AC alternator. In Europe the trend seems to favour smaller diameter, multi-bladed alternator types. In the U.S. they seem to go for large diameter, two or three-bladed versions that perform better at lower wind speeds – the quaintly named 'WindBugger' being a good example. Their output varies a lot, from small vertical-axis ones designed for trickle charging, to large propeller-type ones that can produce up to 30Ah.

Small diameter, multi-bladed wind generator

Large diameter, two-bladed wind generator

Solar Panels

'Fit 'em and forget 'em' goes the sales pitch. 'Free electricity from the sun' claim the advertisements.

"A miracle," say I, in agreement with all apart from the 'free' bit, remembering what it cost to buy two 85 watt panels for *Alacazam*.

A number of factors affect their performance or, from another point of view, just one – the sun:

- Angle of incidence of the sun's rays: This of course depends on season and latitude. At the equator the sun is high in the sky for much of the day, so excellent performance can be expected. In high latitudes, with the sun low in the sky, performance will be much reduced.
- Period of exposure: At the equator, cloud cover excepted, you can feel entitled to 12 hours of it. At high latitudes in the summer, rather more. But in these latitudes in the winter, you shouldn't expect much from your solar panels at all.
- Temperature: As temperature rises, output falls. Output is normally quoted at 25°C. In the sun-drenched tropics their surface temperature could easily be double that and, were it not for the cooling trade winds, their output would be seriously impaired.
- Cloud cover. No surprises there:

A solar cell consists of two layers of silicon deliberately doped with impurities. This makes it a 'semiconductor' in which one of the layers is positive, the other negative. When subjected to the sun's rays, the photovoltaic activity between the two produces an electrical current. The principle's not new, having been unearthed by the French scientist Henri Becquerel (1852–1908), who also won the Nobel Prize for bringing radioactivity to the world's attention.

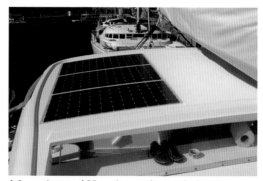

A 3-panel array of 85w solar panels on a doghouse

There are various types of solar cell types – monocrystalline, polycrystalline and amorphous silicon being the most common. Rigid, monocrystalline panels outperform both polycrystalline and flexible amorphous silicon panels. But flexible panels shouldn't be discounted; after all, you can fix them to a non-rigid surface – on a bimini, a curved coachroof or even around a sailcover – where you otherwise couldn't harvest any energy from the sun at all.

Often you'll see rigid panels mounted on pivoting clamps that can be adjusted to be perpendicular to the sun's rays. This will clearly maximise their performance, providing they are regularly adjusted to keep pace with the sun's movement – a degree of discipline that I sadly lack, so mine stay fixed flat on the stern gantry.

Towed Generators

The components of a towed generator (a.k.a. water turbine) are an impellor, 20m to 30m of rotating towline coupled to a pulpit-mounted generator from which a cable delivers the charge to the batteries. Towed generators typically produce around 5A at 6 knots. They really score over their wind-driven brethren in light wind conditions, or on long downwind passages where a wind generator would be seriously impaired by the lack of relative wind. In such situations a towed generator will continue to churn out the amps. They have a keen following in many long-distance blue water sailors, but they do have their own problems:

- Drag. They will typically take between ⅓ and ½ knot off your speed.
- At speeds much above 7 knots they tend to skip along the surface, generating nothing but disappointment. This can be compensated to a degree by adding sinker weights to the impellor, and/or using a longer than standard towline. Some manufacturers offer an alternative coarser-pitched unit which is good for speeds up to 12 knots, but at 6 knots this version will only be generating around half of what the standard unit would.
- In heavy seas they can leap out of the water, where the spinning tow rope is likely to snarl up into some impressive kinks and twists.
- Sharks have been known to consider the impellor as part of their diet.

You should forget about trolling a fishing line when you're towing one of these. The resulting tangle has to be seen to be believed.

Combined Wind/Towed Generators

Towed generators are not much use at anchor, but some manufacturers have overcome this limitation by making them convertible from water to wind mode and vice-versa.

Effect of Solar and Wind Energy on Engine Charging

Here, as I bang away on the laptop at anchor in Antigua, *Alacazam's* solar panels are currently producing around 8A and the wind generator is producing around 5A in the steady 15-knot trade winds. My average power consumption at anchor is around 130Ah – so I hardly ever need to run the engine to charge the AGM batteries. But let's see how the charge periods in our example would be affected by the addition of a solar and wind system similar to *Alacazam's*.

Over a day the solar panels produce around 60Ah and the wind generator around 100Ah. In total let's say 150Ah, and assume that we can find this both at anchor and under way. In our example then, the daily under way drawdown to be made up by the alternator is reduced from 306Ah to 156Ah and at anchor from 212Ah to 62Ah. Running through the calculations again indicates that under way we'd have to run the engine every 31 hours for 1 hour, and at anchor every 3 days for 1 hour. Now that's more like it!

GOING ALOFT

S ome years ago I watched, open-mouthed with a degree of trepidation, as my pal Johnno shinned to the top of my mast using nothing but his hands and bare feet. The spreaders and shroud attachments hardly slowed him down. He wasn't a sailor or a rock climber, but he was a judo expert – and a bit fit with it.

"While you're up there can you take the tricolour lens off and check the bulb?" I asked, from a position some distance from his likely point of impact.

"Er, no," he said, after a brief period of flapping around one-handed.

"That's why I don't climb up that way," I said. Yet every offshore yacht should have some means of going aloft, whether simply to check it, make adjustments to the rigging, or perform repairs or maintenance to the electrics up there – often quite a lot of it.

Safer, more practical methods than that employed by my agile pal include:

- Having someone haul you up on a bosun's chair
- Using mast-steps
- Using a ladder
- Using rope-climbing gear
- Using a hoist

The Bosun's Chair

The most basic type is little more than a short plank, supported by a pair of rope bridles. This type is highly regarded by some old salts as the most practical of all. It may be, but, with little to stop you sliding off it, it's not the safest of designs.

Canvas models, which you sit in rather than on, offer a little more security and generally come equipped with side pockets and clips for tools and equipment. For those who prefer a rigid seat, some are designed with the option of inserting a wooden one.

If, rather than relying entirely on your winchman, you prefer to take an active part in clambering aloft, then the new-generation mast-climbing harnesses are an improvement on the conventional bosun's chair. These types, which incorporate a waist strap and leg straps, allow you full use of your arms and legs while removing any chance of tipping out.

A modern bosun's chair with pockets for tools. Note the safety halyard – always a sensible precaution

Fig.14.1

Mast climbing harnesses give you more scope for movement when aloft

Mast Steps

If your cruising takes you to the tropics, it's handy to have mast-steps up to the first set of spreaders from where, with the sun over your shoulder, you can spot the coral reefs. It's always useful to have a couple at the top of the mast for support when you're working up there, so it doesn't take a great leap of imagination to fit them in the intervening mast section. This is how *Alacazam* ended up with a full set of folding steps made from a lightweight nylon/GRP composite – which, most importantly, don't rattle.

Rigid steps, convenient inasmuch as you don't have to open them on the way up or close them on the way down, create additional windage and are prone to hooking up sheets and halyards when you'd rather they didn't. In high winds they can be noisy.

Mast steps provide a convenient and always available means of going aloft

Ladders

Conventional rope ladders with wooden rungs have been largely replaced by much lighter versions fabricated from webbing strap with carbon fibre rung inserts. They're deployed on a halyard hoisted to the masthead and secured at the foot of the mast. Even so, they must be strapped to the mast at a couple of points to stop them swinging about.

Another design incorporates foot loops and is hoisted up the mainsail track. The loop should be reinforced to reduce the pinching force on your feet – you'll find deck shoes will help too. Before buying one of these, you should check that it will fit your track or mast groove. Of course, if you've got an in-mast furling mainsail then this type of ladder isn't for you. Similarly, if your reason for going up the mast is to investigate a mainsail that refuses to come down there's not much point in getting the ladder out of its bag, unless you've got a separate mast track.

Rope Climbing Gear

Rock climbers and mountaineers have been using this type of equipment for years, although the purists among them may tell you it's cheating. At the centre of this system is the jumar – a one-way, hand-operated rope jammer – or in the case of the 'TopClimber', two of them. This device consists of two parts – a bosun's chair with a backrest and a jumar, together with webbing foot loops and a second jumar. The whole arrangement is set up on a taut halyard attached to the deck.

With one of these you can shin up the mast like a monkey up a stick, by alternately standing up on the leg straps, then sliding the bosun's chair jumar up the rope, then sitting into the bosun's chair, which allows you to slide up the foot loop jumar, then standing up on the foot loops. Repeat the process until you find yourself at the masthead, and reverse the procedure to get back down.

Hoists

There are two types, one of which is based on chain-hoist principles, the other a two-part tackle. Both types of unit are first hauled to the top of the mast, and the user – installed in a bosun's chair – pulls himself up, assisted by the mechanical advantage provided by the hoist. The chain-hoist type, of which the 'MastLift' is an example, provides a mechanical advantage of 10:1 by pulling on one rope with the descent managed by pulling on another. The two-part tackle version, like the 'EZ Climber', provides, as you may have guessed, a mechanical advantage of 2:1, although additional block kits will increase this to 5:1. Descent is managed by an internal friction brake, backed up by a jumar attached by a lanyard to the bosun's chair, which will save the day if you should inadvertently let go of the rope.

Whichever approach you use to climb the mast, a chest harness secured to a separate halyard and controlled by a member of your crew will provide security in the event of the unexpected.

15 ANCHORING & MOORING

G iven the choice of an expensive marina berth, picking up a mooring of unknown condition or laying to their own ground tackle, most cruising sailors will take the latter option unless some overriding requirement demands otherwise. However, if the skipper is to sleep soundly at night he'll need to be confident that the yacht is properly anchored – and when later left unattended, will still be where he left it when he returns.

Securing a yacht to the seabed isn't something to be taken lightly. As a general rule, ground tackle should be as heavy as the boat (and crew) can reasonably manage and, if it's to do as intended, properly deployed.

Incidentally, if you use a 35lb anchor, an 8mm chain, never anchor in more than 15m and are reasonably sound in body and mind, then you can probably manage with a manual windlass. If any of those conditions are exceeded you'll really appreciate an electric one.

A 45lb Bruce anchor stowed in the stemhead fitting

Most of us stow our bower anchor in the stemhead fitting when on all but the longest passages, but it's a mistake to rely on the windlass to hold it securely in place there when under way. A good friend of mine, who's sailed enough miles to know better, did just that. Battling against wind and current through the Anegada Passage on passage for the island of St Maarten he thought he heard a rumble from forward. Everything seemed okay so he thought nothing more of it – until he went to drop the hook in Simpson Bay Lagoon. The rumble he heard was a 65lb Bruce and 100m of 10mm chain responding to the forces of gravity. He always lashes his anchor firmly in place now.

If we were to have just one anchor aboard, with a reasonable chance of it grabbing a hold in most types of seabed, then a 'fisherman' type would probably be the best bet. These, though, are seldom the cruising sailor's preferred choice, for a number of good reasons:

- If the boat swings to wind or current, the chain is likely to foul the protruding fluke.
- It won't stow in the stemhead.
- For the anchor to be of sufficient weight it will be physically large.
- The stock being at 90° to the flukes makes it an awkward brute to wrestle over the stemhead.

Most offshore boats are equipped with at least two anchors (each with their own separate rodes), a plough or spade type being the preferred choice for the bower, and possibly a Danforth type as a kedge. In spite of its awkwardness, it's no bad thing to have a disassembled fisherman anchor stowed wherever you can find space for it.

Modern plough and spade-type anchors are designed to bury themselves completely. For this to happen, the burying force applied by the rode must be horizontal. When increasing the horizontal force to the point that the anchor drags, it will do so by ploughing along below the seabed. This is not good, as sooner or later it will meet a change in seabed conditions and break out. With anchors of the same type, the larger versions will always require a progressively greater horizontal force before they start to drag. Hence, big is best. Size *does* matter.

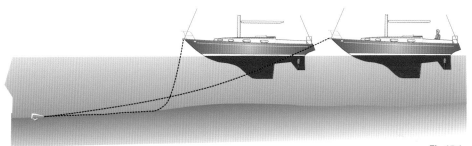

Fig.15.1

So for the anchor to work as it should, the pull on it must be horizontal, i.e. the end of the rode must remain lying on the seabed. But if we haven't deployed enough of it, it won't be. As we all know, to weigh anchor we shorten the scope, thereby increasing the angle of the rode at the anchor to the point at which it rotates and breaks free, enabling us to haul it aboard. This angle has been found to be around 15° to 20° for most anchors. So when we want the anchor to stay put, we need to be sure that this critical angle isn't reached. Take a look at fig. 15.1. Here a boat is anchored in 10m of water, and the rode is tight with no catenary.

The scope can be expressed in terms of the critical angle (θ) and the depth as:

Scope $= 10m/\sin\theta$

Which for 15° $= 38.6m$, and for 20° $= 29.2m$

Or Scope/Depth Ratio at 15° is 3.86:1, and at 20° $= 2.92:1$

Taking the worst case, the minimum Scope/Depth Ratio to ensure the critical angle isn't reached should be 4:1 – not 3:1 as is often quoted for an all-chain rode. Remember that this is the length of the submerged rode; if you're measuring scope at the bow roller add 2m or so (the height of the stemhead above the waterline) to the actual depth before applying the 4:1 rule – or make it 5:1 to be on the safe side.

The Rode – Chain or Rope?

The bar-taut rode in fig. 15.1 is clearly undesirable, but it's a lot more readily achieved with an all-rope rode than an all-chain one.

Chain, having a much higher density than rope, falls naturally into a gravity-assisted catenary from the bow roller, which resists the tendency to straighten out. This serves two functions. It applies a force in the chain opposing the wind-load on the boat, and it absorbs energy when the boat surges back in gusts. Of course, a 10mm chain will apply more opposing force and absorb more energy than an 8mm one. Once again, big is best.

Let's go back to the bar-taut situation for a moment. Here the chain has lost its energy-absorbing catenary, so any further load from a gust or a wave striking the bow will be applied directly to the anchor. Such shock loads can be enormous, and are almost bound to cause the anchor to drag and ultimately break out. But in the same situation an all-rope rode will absorb such shock loads due to its lower modulus of elasticity – it stretches more. But that's not to say an all-rope rode is better than chain. It isn't; the required scope to avoid the bar-taut situation will be much more than for chain – and one nick from a piece of coral on the seabed and it's game over.

An All-Chain Rode

With no wind, current or waves the anchor chain will hang vertically from the bow roller. As the wind picks up, the yacht will drift back, lifting as it does so just enough chain from the seabed for the catenary force to balance the load applied by the wind. As the wind increases further, more chain will be lifted until the point is reached where only a few links remain on the seabed. This is the boundary condition, and is the limit for safe anchoring with an all-chain rode; any further increase in tension and the chain will start to snatch at the anchor – with predictable results.

The solution of course is to let out more chain – but how much? Well, that depends on a number of factors, i.e.:

- How hard you expect the wind to blow
- The depth of water you're anchored in
- How heavy your chain is
- How big your boat is

There are more mathematical formulae that could help us make our decisions but, in the real world of cruising, there's rarely the time for such luxuries. Fortunately, over the centuries rules of thumb have been developed to help us with any dilemmas.

This first and, as I've already mentioned, most commonly quoted in the UK, is that we should range out a length of chain equal to at least three times the maximum depth of water, which usually means at high tide. Now, this might be sufficient in the glutinous mud so typical of British anchorages but would be woefully inadequate in some other circumstances. For instance, in the Mediterranean – into which only a few major rivers flow – there is very little mud. A typical anchorage is likely to be sandy and, moreover, much of that sand is going to be very light, having been wind-blown from the Sahara. There, not even 4:1 is considered secure. Indeed, the custom is to let out at least five times the depth of water – tides not being a consideration in that region.

The wise skipper will remember that an anchor rode is useless slumbering in the chain locker. Only once it's deployed will it do its job and keep you safe. The sensible thing to do is always err on the generous side and let out as much chain as each circumstance reasonably allows.

Snubbers

If you haven't got sufficient chain aboard to deploy the indicated scope length, you should set a second anchor or use a snubber to absorb the additional loadings. The best material for a snubber is 14mm to 20mm diameter nylon rope – 3-strand is fine, but better still is multiplait. For it to work properly as a spring it needs to be at least 10m to 15m long, attached to the chain with either a rolling hitch or a chain hook, with the other end secured to a strongpoint on deck. It won't reduce the ultimate load on the anchor, but it will greatly reduce the severity of the snatching.

A Chain-to-Rope Rode

Let's assume that wherever you can you anchor in around 6m of water. The 5:1 rule says you need to deploy 30m of chain in moderate winds. A good compromise is to have this length of chain attached to around 100m of nylon rode, either 3-strand or multi-plait. Either type splices neatly into the chain links, as shown in fig 170/1, with little if any loss of strength, but the spliced part may require some help over the anchor windlass. Most of the time you'll be anchored on an all-chain rode, but when you need more scope you'll have lots of nice stretchy nylon rode to absorb the shock-loads. A tip – have a few metres of chain attached at the other end on the rode. If, in extreme conditions, you ever have to deploy it all, you'll have chain going over the bow roller where chafe would otherwise be a major risk. You'll not be short of other things to worry about.

Rope to chain splice

Anchors

There's been something of a revolution in anchor technology in recent years. The old guard have been challenged by a new generation of young upstarts, the main contenders being Spade, Rocna and Bugel (a.k.a. Wasi in the USA).

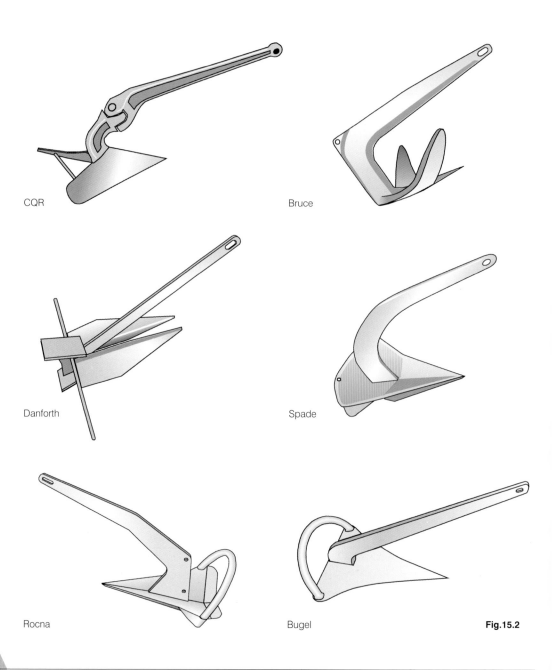

CQR

Bruce

Danforth

Spade

Rocna

Bugel

Fig.15.2

The four principal performance criteria we demand from our anchor are:

1. **It must dig in fast every time** – If it doesn't it will have a chance to collect weed before it starts to penetrate the seabed.
2. **It must bury deep** – The deeper it buries, the greater the mass of seabed above and ahead of the anchor – the cone of resistance – and therefore the greater the holding power.
3. **It must provide high holding power** – Holding power is achieved as a result of surface area, blade profile and the depth to which the anchor has buried. But given sufficient load, all anchors will eventually drag. Those anchors that remain buried while dragging, rather than capsizing and pulling out, are clearly preferable.

   The static holding power (the resistance provided before the anchor starts to drag in sand) appears to be no more than 20 times the anchor weight, and sometimes as little as 10 times for a less-efficient anchor. This varies with the nature of the seabed. So if you use a 15kg anchor, its static hold is unlikely to be greater than 300kgf. For a 10m yacht this is the force which is likely to be experienced in a 40-knot wind, and for a 12m yacht in a 33-knot wind.
4. **It must hold in wind or current shifts** – A real test of an anchor occurs when the wind shifts or the tide turns. In these conditions some types have a tendency to roll and pull out rather than drag around to face the new direction, and others that have failed to bury themselves completely and leave bits sticking above the seabed are likely to be tripped.

To a greater or lesser extent, all the anchors mentioned above – old guard and new generation – meet these requirements, but some perform better in certain types of seabed than others. For example, the Danforth is as good as any in sand, although there is a risk of it rolling and pulling out as the tide turns; and nothing beats a Fisherman in rock or kelp.

But there has been some advanced thinking in the design of the new-generation anchors, as a result of which they all provide excellent holding power, and are generally more reliable in their deployment:

- If they land upside down, they immediately turn right way up ready for immediate penetration as the load comes on the chain. The Spade achieves this through weight distribution and an angled ballast chamber, the similar Sword by a combination of shank and blade curves, and both the Rocna and the Bugel by a roll-bar.
- They dig in very quickly – the Spade in particular is said to do so within its own length.
- They completely bury themselves in most seabed conditions and re-align quickly with changes in wind and tide without pulling free.

For anyone contemplating the purchase of a new anchor, they should have a serious look at one of these.

A further consideration could be one of the lightweight Danforth look-a-likes, of which the Fortress is probably the best known. They can be completely dismantled and make an excellent choice for a kedge, their light weight enabling you to go up a size or two over a steel Danforth of the same weight for increased holding power.

Mooring Warp

Commercial mooring buoys either have a pick-up line attached to a heavy mooring warp, or will be of the type that requires you to attach your own line through a ring in the top. For the latter, it's very handy to have aboard a rope-chain-rope warp made up as shown in the picture to the right. This will eliminate any possibility of chafe that may otherwise occur. If you use one of the boathooks with an automatic line threader, a light line spliced to one of the end loops in the warp can make mooring to a buoy a very slick operation.

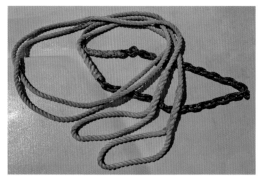

Rope/chain/rope warp for mooring to buoy

Roll Stabilisers

Anchored or moored, with the wind and swell coming from different directions, you'll roll. Gently is tolerable, soporific even. Anything more is a real pain, and can be downright dangerous, particularly for the cook. One way to calm things down is with a roll stabiliser, or flopper stopper as they're often called. Essentially this is a drag device suspended over the beam on either the boom or a spinnaker pole. As the boat rolls the device is dragged upwards through the water where its drag slows the roll down. Good designs rapidly sink as the boat rolls back, and perform again. Less efficient models flutter around at the top of the roll and have little effect.

One type available commercially is moulded in plastic and looks like a sombrero. These perform best when fixed in series, with a large weight suspended below.

A very efficient device can be made from a triangular sheet of fibreglass or aluminium, as shown in the picture to the right. The elegance of this design is that it presents maximum surface area (and hence maximum drag) on the way up and, as it dives on its weighted corner, the minimum on the way down.

Another approach is a design by Magma Products Inc., who manufacture a rectangular (975mm x 525mm) stainless steel model called the 'Rock-n-Roll Stabilizer' which is hinged down its longitudinal centreline. This allows the device to collapse as it returns under its own weight to its operating depth, and enables it to be stowed unobtrusively below when not in use.

THE TENDER

16

Whatever your preference for a tender is, one of the first things you'll have to think about is what to do with it on passage. The options are:

- Stow it below
- Stow it on deck
- Hang it in davits on the stern
- Tow it astern

It's when you start looking at these options that your choice of the compromise dinghy – for that's what it will be for all but owners of large yachts – will become apparent.

Stow below – The best solution, but only really an option for 'roll-up' inflatables or collapsible rigid dinghies unless your yacht is large enough to sport a transom garage.

Stow on deck – On most yachts there's room to lash a tender upside-down on the foredeck. On larger yachts a better location is aft of the mast on the coachroof. Either way, your vision ahead will be restricted and on an offshore passage where a boarding sea is always a possibility, the security of any such arrangement may be tested severely. Permanently installed chocks and appropriately positioned strong-points to lash down to are a must.

Hang it in davits – Definitely the least troublesome solution, and fine for coastal hops. But for an offshore passage it would be not without some risk.

Towed astern – With the outboard motor removed, rigid dinghies tow well. RIBs (Rigid Inflatable Boats) do too, but with a lot more resistance. Again, towing is fine for coastal hops in good conditions, but is clearly an unsuitable approach for an offshore passage. The light weight of inflatables enables them to fly like a kite when towed astern in a strong wind. Huge fun for onlookers, but not quite so entertaining for the crew. It's something that happens to most of us early in our sailing careers – and just the once.

Dinghy Choice

Whether it's an inflatable, a RIB or a rigid dinghy, one thing's for certain – it will get some abuse. It will be dragged up stony beaches; left to bounce around on the dinghy dock; chafe against harbour walls and spend most of its life in the harsh sunlight. Durability is a key requirement.

A crowded dinghy dock in Nelson's Dockyard, Antigua

Inflatables – These are stable craft and have good load-carrying ability, but the cheapest versions are so lacking in durability that they're not worth considering. Versions made of PVC fabric will suffer from ultra-violet degradation, particularly so in the tropics – even if the tubes are fitted with a protective canvas cover they'll do well to last more than a couple of seasons. In hot climates the harsh sunlight will destroy all but those made from UV-resistant Hypalon® polyester reinforced fabric.

Compared to rigid dinghies, inflatables don't row very well at all, but those with inflatable keels have much better directional stability than the flat-bottomed variety. With a sufficiently powerful outboard these keeled types will plane, which is more fuel-efficient than chugging along in displacement mode.

The inflatable keel is held in position by a floor which will be either of interlocking ply panels (heavy, and awkward to stow), plywood slats (which will conveniently roll up with the dinghy) or a removable inflatable floor. My choice would be the latter; it's the lightest solution and adds rigidity to the dinghy. A 3m version equipped with a 6hp engine can easily be carried up the beach by two adults – an important feature in my book. All inflatables have a notable ability to slop water over the tubes when under way, often in sufficient quantity to dampen anyone's spirits.

RIBs (Rigid Inflatable Boats) – Along with their higher price, it's the rigid hull that distinguishes these from their inflatable cousins. Heavier but more stable than an inflatable, these can quickly be brought onto the plane by a suitably sized outboard. A big plus is that the hydro-dynamically efficient hulls throw the water aside, away from the tubes. Now you have a sporting chance of delivering your beloved ashore in a similarly pristine condition to that in which she set out.

RIBs are particularly well suited for snorkelling or scuba-diving excursions away from the yacht, where their high stability allows a reasonably fit and agile diver to clamber back aboard unassisted. The rest of us though may need a short rope ladder.

The hull material is either GRP or aluminium. My preference would be for one of the aluminium models, which are considerably lighter than their GRP counterparts, and more resistant to damage when dragged over a rocky beach.

For stowing on deck, a RIB can have its tubes deflated and tucked inside its hull, making it much less cumbersome and offering less resistance to a boarding sea.

Rigid dinghies – For robustness, you can't beat a rigid dinghy. Made of wood, GRP or aluminium, they're less expensive than a similarly sized inflatable. Kits are commercially available for those who wish to build their own, usually in either marine ply or cedar strip.

Positive buoyancy is achieved either by building in airtight flotation chambers in the bow and stern seats, or by using expanded polyurethane foam between the outer hull and an inner skin. The latter approach adds strength, but more weight. And if you damage the hull and saturate the foam, a lot more weight. Rigid dinghies aren't as stable as inflatables so won't appeal as much to snorkelers or scuba divers, although stability can be improved by the addition of a flotation collar.

A well-designed one will be a joy to row and, provided you've invested in a good pair of oars and enjoy a bit of exercise, you may decide that you can manage without the expense of an outboard motor. Some manufacturers offer a sailing option incorporating a mast, centre-board and rudder. While you shouldn't expect Admiral's Cup performance from a small sailing dinghy designed primarily as a work horse, the simplicity of this arrangement will appeal to many offshore cruisers.

A sailing inflatable dinghy

17 PROPELLERS & THINGS

It would be nice to think we only use our engines for getting in and out of harbour and topping up the batteries. But when the wind is being unco-operative – not enough of it, or blowing from where we want to go – then many of us drop the headsail and motor or motorsail towards our destination. The point at which we do so is a personal decision. Some of us only resort to it after the spinnaker has collapsed lifeless and deflated onto the foredeck, while others cheerfully turn on if they can't fetch their destination on one tack. Skippers of older yachts with single-cylinder long-stroke thumpers may be more reluctant to do so than those with modern high-revving but quieter, vibration-free installations – but sooner or later...

Having made the decision to motor you might as well get a move on, so a nice big propeller is the thing to have. But what about the drag it creates when under sail? The drag created by a fixed three-bladed prop is considerable. Although the drag of a fixed twin-bladed prop can be reduced somewhat by lining it up vertically so that it's in the turbulence aft of the keel, if you're at all interested in performance under sail there's little option but to spring for a folding or feathering propeller.

In light airs one of these low-drag props can offer a dramatic increase in speed under sail, typically around half to a full knot – maybe 1½ knots in light airs. They're not cheap, but usually represent the best performance gain per pound sterling when considered against other possible speed-seeking expenditure on rig or sail modifications. Let's take a look at the benefits and disadvantages of both types:

Folding Propellers

On these, the blades are pivoted and fold backwards under the force of the water flow when not in use. It's often necessary to put the engine in gear to stop the shaft from turning, which will get the blades to close.

A 3-bladed folding prop

Benefits	Disadvantages
• Very low drag characteristics	• Astern performance compromised due to the centripetal force required to hold the blades open being opposed by the thrust of the blades pulling the boat astern
• When folded, won't get hooked up on ropes or other floating flotsam and jetsam	
• Simpler design, hence lower purchase price than the feathering type	• Tendency to wear quicker than feathering type
	• Pitch of the blades is fixed

Feathering Propellers

An internal mechanism turns the blade's edge into the water flow to minimise drag when under sail. As engine power is applied, the blades are turned into the required position for forward or reverse propulsion. Most feathering propellers have a pitch-adjustment mechanism that allows adjustment of the propeller to the optimum pitch for the vessel. Some feature external pitch adjusters, which give simple access to the adjustment for forward and reverse independently. Forward can be set for optimum motoring performance and reverse can be set for best manoeuverability and thrust – handy when trying to back off a sandbank, or bringing the boat to a rapid stop.

A 3-bladed feathering prop

Rope cutter

Benefits	Disadvantages
• Adjustable pitch offers optimum performance both forward and astern	• High price
• Much lower drag than a fixed prop	• Slightly more drag than a folding prop
• More robust construction than a folding prop	• More likely to foul ropes or nets when feathered

Long-keel boats, where the prop is located in an aperture, are unlikely to have room for a folding prop; a fixed or feathering type is their only option.

Whichever type of prop you choose, a rope cutter fitted just forward of it may well turn out to be a wise investment.

18

SPARES & CONSUMABLES

I t's said that the only way to be sure of having sufficient spares to hand is to tow an identical yacht astern. Not a very practical solution, but Murphy's Law dictates that you'll otherwise have a spare part for everything but for the thing that's broken. Modern cruising boats are much more complex machines than they were a generation ago – it's impossible to have a spare aboard for everything, irrespective of the size of your boat and the depth of your pocket. But conversely, the popularity of recreational sailing has led to the spread of chandlers and specialised service centres along most of the popular world cruising routes, and if your required bit isn't in stock it won't take long to get it brought in. Reassuring to a degree, but Murphy is more inclined to amuse himself when you're far offshore rather than conveniently close to a well-equipped chandlery.

So, starting with the premise that you can't have a spare for everything, how do you decide exactly what to take aboard? That of course would be easy if you knew what was going to break. The best you can do is to form an opinion as to what parts of your boat are most vulnerable to loss or damage through accident or general wear and tear, and what the consequences of such failure would be. Only then will you be able to address objectively the issue of what spares to have aboard. Could you live with the problem until you reach shoreside facilities, or would it need fixing at sea?

An established project management technique will help you. A tad ponderous perhaps, but effective. It works like this:

1. Develop a risk register – a brief description of which appears here with a fuller explanation in the Appendix starting on page 158. This is a list of all the things that could fail on your boat – it will be a long one. You'll find it convenient to group them under headings – sails, rigging, engine, deck gear, domestic, etc – and rationalise them into sub-groups, before moving on to the next step.

2. Evaluate each item on the list in terms of its:

   • Probability of occurrence, rated as low (very unlikely to happen), medium (a fair chance of this happening) or high (almost a certainty), and

   • Impact, similarly rated as low (not important, won't affect much if it happens), medium (this would need fixing) or high (a serious problem, could curtail the voyage).

3. You'll now be able to categorise each risk as to its overall severity, combining probability and impact, where:

- A Category 1 risk (High Probability/High Impact) represents an unacceptable risk event – the ultimate 'show-stopper'. If you have one of these in your risk register you shouldn't go to sea before taking measures as necessary to reduce either its probability of occurrence or its impact – or both. To take a rather daft example, if you only have one winch handle aboard the odds are you'll lose it over the side at some stage – a high probability – and its loss would have a high impact. You need a couple of spares.
- Category 2 to 6 risks represent manageable risk events in diminishing levels of severity,
- Category 7 risks (Low Probability/Low Impact) represent an inconsequential risk event which could be tolerated.

In assessing 'Probability of Occurrence', age and condition of the parts associated with the risk event will to a large extent decide how you rate it, as will the duration of your intended voyage.

Clearly, if your standing rigging is new, the risk of shroud failure will be lower than if it was 10 or 12 years old. In this latter situation, a prudent skipper planning an ocean crossing may well decide to mitigate the risk by replacing all – or some – of it. Even so, he's still likely to carry a few short lengths of appropriately sized rigging wire, together with bulldog grips, shackles, cringles and Sta-Lock® (or Norseman®) terminals. Similarly, in assessing 'Impact', circumstances will affect the rating. A shroud failure will be rated 'high' wherever and whenever it occurs, but a toilet pump failure on a channel crossing will have much less of an impact for a single-hander than for a fully crewed yacht halfway across the Pacific.

Having gone through this analysis you can now apply a degree of objectivity to what spares you should carry on board. Obviously all 'High Risk' items (Categories 1 to 3) must be catered for in depth, as these will be the ones that would seriously affect your progress and safety on the voyage, whereas you may feel that fewer spares are required for 'Medium Risk' items (Categories 4 and 5), and maybe none at all for 'Low Risk' items (Categories 6 and 7), these being minor inconveniences that could be lived with until your arrival in port.

An extract from a Risk Register is shown in fig. 18.1.

Risk Item	Probability			Impact			Risk Category
	High	Med	Low	High	Med	Low	
SAILS & RIGGING							
Halyard breaks		✓		✓			2
Sail rips		✓		✓			2
Reefing line fails		✓			✓		3
Rigging screw fails			✓	✓			3
Shroud breaks			✓	✓			3
Furling gear jams			✓	✓			3
POWER SUPPLY							
Fuse blows		✓					2

Fig.18.1

Repair or Replace?

Should you carry a second entire unit for a small item –
a galley foot pump for example – or a service kit for it?
Or both? Stowage space will be key considerations here,
but the best answer is probably both. For example, the
galley foot pump could be repaired with a service pack,
but at sea it's easier (and a whole lot quicker) to replace
it with a new one, and use the service pack later to create
another 'new' one. This dual approach lends itself to
most manual pumps – including in particular the pump
unit of the sea toilet. And whatever the risk rating, if the
spare item is small and cheap, buy two of them.

System Redundancy

Where an essential system is too sophisticated for repair by a normally skilled mortal, a back-up
system (or a series of them) must be available to turn to in the event of failure. A good example would
be the failure of your primary navigation system. If this is a fully integrated chart plotter it should be
backed up by an independent GPS unit – either fixed or hand-held, or one of each – and paper charts.
The longstop in this chain of redundancy would be your sextant, complete with reduction tables and
an almanac – and even these can be backed up with electronic programmes and tables on your
laptop computer. Your fixed VHF radio can be supplemented by a hand-held unit, which will be a
handy item to carry on dinghy trips and a valuable inclusion in the emergency grab bag. If your hand-
bearing compass is the type that can be secured in a bulkhead-mounted bracket, it will supplement
the steering compass. I still have aboard a Walker towed log with a couple of spare spinners, a relic
retained when I sold *Jalingo*, but sound insurance against losing both the GPS and the thru-hull log
unit. And when the depth sounder fails as you're approaching the anchorage, a leadline is just what
you'll need.

SAFETY & EMERGENCY EQUIPMENT

There's no doubt that offshore sailing can be a hazardous business, not just in heavy weather when our awareness of the risks is at its peak, but also in less testing conditions when we may let our guard down.

The risks can be categorised as:

- Those associated with the vessel itself, i.e. fire and flood, either of which may result in its total loss.
- Those associated with the crew, i.e. man overboard, personal injury or illness.

Good seamanship from the skipper and crew goes a long way towards risk avoidance, but it remains the skipper's responsibility to ensure that all appropriate safety precautions are taken in respect of himself, his crew and his boat.

Good preparation is everything. Once you're way offshore, it's too late to start wishing you'd had the liferaft serviced, the fire extinguishers recharged, or the out-of-date flares replaced. With a full-on emergency you can only use what you've got to hand – and it had better work first time, and be where everyone can find it fast.

Let's start with a couple of emergencies that we can do much to avoid completely – being run down by a larger vessel, or falling over the side.

Be Seen and Heard

- The regulation SOLAS V/19 requires all small craft to fit a radar reflector 'if practicable', fitted or hoisted to at least 5m above the deck. Radar reflectors come in one of two types – passive or active. The majority of reflectors seen on sailing boats are of the passive type that operate by reflecting incoming radar energy back from whence it came. There are several designs available – some good, others next to useless. If you decide on an octahedral type, it should have a diagonal measurement of at least 450mm. Any reflector other than octahedral should have a documented RCS (radar cross-section) of not less than 10m^2. So choose with care and, when you get the opportunity, ask a radar-equipped vessel to confirm just how effective your choice was.

- Active radar reflectors – sometimes more accurately referred to as radar target enhancers – are electronic devices that must be hooked up to your boat's 12v supply. In simple terms these types receive an incoming radar signal, amplify it electronically, then squirt it back so that the transmitting vessel sees a greatly enhanced target on its radar screen. They are fairly considerate of your batteries, typically consuming 150mA in standby mode, and 350mA when awoken from their slumber by an incoming radar signal. If you install an active radar reflector and a class B AIS transponder as described on page 100, then you've done pretty much everything that you can to make yourself visible in poor conditions. Except, maybe, for hull colour. Most GRP-hulled boats hatch from their moulds sporting a white gelcoat, which, in a lively sea – and together with white sails – is probably the best marine camouflage going.
- Make sure that your navigation lights comply with the requirements set out in the 'International Regulations for the Prevention of Collision at Sea', and carry spare bulbs for each light.
- A 12v high-powered searchlight of around a million candlepower or more, shone directly at the bridge of a ship (or onto your sails) may get their attention.
- Have a compressed-air foghorn aboard – a puny squawk in comparison to the big ship versions – but better than nothing.

Don't Fall Off

- Provide harnesses and lifejackets for all members of the crew.
- Fit pad-eyes for hooking on in the cockpit, and provide jackstays along port and starboard side decks.

Emergency Equipment

An offshore boat must be equipped to deal with the following emergencies:

Flooding

Bilge Pumps – Ideally, the manual bilge pump in the cockpit will be supplemented by a second one below decks, both capable of being independently operated with the hatches closed. Unless permanently fitted, the handles should be secured with a lanyard and stored nearby. An electric, float-switch controlled bilge pump should also be fitted.

Softwood bungs – It's good practice to have one of these of appropriate size attached to each thru-hull fitting by a short lanyard so you can close it off in the event of failure.

Buckets – At least two – rubber ones rather than the less robust plastic variety – each of around 2 gallons capacity.

Fire

Fire extinguishers – At least two multi-purpose extinguishers are required, located near the galley, the engine and the electrical switch panel. For more information on fire fighting, visit http://www.rya.org.uk /infoadvice/regssafety/Equipment/Pages/fire.aspx.

Fire blanket – Fitted in its quick-release container close to the galley.

Correct! Fingers protected.

Wrong! Fingers could be burnt.

First Aid and Medical

At least one of the crew should have attended an RYA First Aid course as run by all RYA recognised training centres.

A comprehensive first aid kit and manual should be carried, and all crew members (it might be the qualified first-aider who's injured) made familiar with the contents of both. As a minimum the kit should contain:

- Bandages and plasters
- Antiseptic cream and ointments
- Eyewash
- Compress
- Inhalants
- Antacids and laxatives
- Paracetomol
- Analgesic
- Dramamine
- Vaseline
- Chap stick
- Sunscreen lotion
- Water purification tablets
- Insect repellent
- Nail clippers
- Scissors
- Tweezers
- Dental floss
- Oil of cloves
- Emergency dental kit

Your local medical centre is a good place to get advice. When we finally cast-off our lines from our Tamar River Sailing Club mooring for long-term cruising in warmer climes, my GP was most helpful as to what medicines and antibiotics should be put aboard, and in what circumstances to use them. If he's a really understanding type – mine served in the Royal Marines – you just might get a prescription. But sailors are a pretty healthy bunch; the odds are that you won't need them.

Man Overboard

Recovery equipment must be within easy reach of the helmsman and should include:

- A heaving line; essentially a 20m length of floating line with a weighted monkey's fist on the end of it.
- A horseshoe lifebuoy equipped with a drogue, a whistle and an automatically activated light, and a danbuoy with a flag.
- A lifesling. This is a flotation harness attached to 50m of floating line. It's kept in a storage bag on the stern rail, with the end of the line attached to a stanchion base or similar strongpoint. On deployment the line remains attached, while the helmsman manoeuvres the boat in decreasing circles until the lifesling is within reach of the casualty. At this point the boat must be stopped and the casualty hauled back to the boat. A halyard can then be attached directly to the harness and the casualty winched back aboard – all in all an experience he's not likely to forget in a hurry.

Calling for Help

Essential equipment for attracting a potential rescuer's attention includes VHF radio, an EPIRB and pyrotechnics (distress flares).

As discussed earlier a DSC-equipped VHF radio makes calling for help a push-button affair. But if your distress situation is the result of the loss of your rig, then your VHF antenna most likely went with it, and any amount of button-pushing will go unheeded. In such an event, an emergency antenna will be much appreciated by all involved.

If your distress call doesn't achieve the desired result, the next stage in this unhappy process will be the deployment of your EPIRB and, ultimately, maybe abandoning ship.

Your flare pack should be stowed in a watertight container and include as a minimum:

- 4 red parachute flares
- 4 red hand-held flares
- 4 white hand-held flares
- 2 orange smoke canisters

An offshore flare pack

Abandoning Ship

In the Fastnet Race of 1979, when freak weather conditions engulfed the fleet in the Western Approaches, 24 yachts were abandoned by their crews who took to liferafts in the belief that their yachts were about to sink. The following day, after the horrendous storm had passed through, 19 of the abandoned yachts were found floating and intact.

Tragically, a number of those who took to their liferaft lost their lives.

Many lessons were learned from the '79 Fastnet, one of which is that we should be absolutely certain that our vessel is about to go down before abandoning ship.

Liferafts designed and approved for offshore or trans-ocean use will typically have two stacked tubes, a double floor, a self-inflating canopy, large ballast pockets and a webbing or rope boarding ladder. Equipment included within the packed liferaft is likely to include:

- A drogue, or sea anchor
- A bailer or small pump
- A heaving line
- A repair kit
- Paddles
- A flare kit
- A waterproof floating torch
- A graduated cup
- Some means of collecting and storing rainwater

This equipment should be supplemented by a readily available 'grab-bag', containing, for example:

- A waterproof hand-held VHF radio
- An EPIRB (transferred from the yacht)
- A supply of drinking water in a sealed container
- A fishing kit
- Sea-sickness tablets
- Non-thirst provoking food rations, and barley sugar sweets or equivalent
- A second drogue and line
- A second waterproof floating torch with spare bulb and batteries
- A floating knife
- A can opener
- A first aid kit
- Chemical lightsticks
- A signalling mirror
- A signalling whistle

Overwhelming Seas

Sailboats aren't designed to take the seas on the beam. It's the pointed end that offers the least exposure to the force of the sea, and it's this knife-like profile that cleaves the sea apart as we move ahead. But a boat is a contrary beast; the first thing that happens when the sails are lowered, steerage is lost or the engine stops, is that she'll fall off the wind and present her vulnerable broadside to the seas. In heavy weather she'll now be wallowing in the troughs, at risk of being laid flat or rolled right over. Lying ahull in such a fashion, once considered an acceptable storm tactic, is now known to be a recipe for disaster. In storm conditions your options are heaving-to or, sea-room permitting, running before it. The recommended practice of heaving-to under sail brings the boat to a near stop, and points the boat obliquely into the approaching waves. Fine for heavy displacement long-keelers, but not so for modern fin-keeled yachts which are often reluctant to heave-to effectively, largely due to their shallow forefoots.

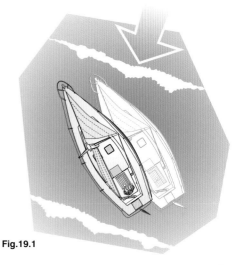

Fig.19.1

With the jib backed and pushing against the mainsail the boat will look after herself

- ## Sea Anchors

  Many offshore sailors now advocate the use of a sea-anchor for heaving-to, which will bring the boat directly into the wind and stop it dead in the water. Often known as para-anchors, they're derived from circular aerial parachutes, and are deployed from the bow on a long rode. The rode is chain-to-nylon rope, but reversed so that the chain is at the bow end. Rigged thus, chafe in the bow roller won't be an issue, and the para-anchor will remain submerged.

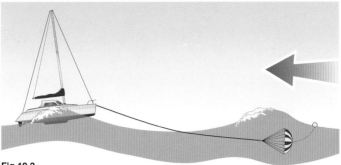

Fig.19.2

To prevent snatching, the rode length should equal wavelength so boat and sea anchor lift and fall at the same time

• Drogues

Running before a full gale on the edge of control may be acceptable for a fully crewed racing yacht, but not so for the likes of us cruisers. The risks are enormous; falling off a crest into the trough may cause huge damage to the hull, and the prospect of being hurled end-over-end – pitchpoling – is almost unthinkable. The boat must be slowed down to a manageable speed of 6 knots or less. Traditionally this was done by towing warps astern to create drag and keep the boat stern-on to the seas.

There are a number of purpose-made drogues of various designs on the market, which when properly deployed have a more predictable and consistent speed-limiting effect than warps. They fall into two basic categories – medium-pull and low-pull devices.

Probably the best known of the medium-pull types is the series drogue, designed by Donald Jordan. It consists of a bridle and a rode with between 100 and 200 125mm diameter cones spliced into the rode at around 500mm intervals. A weight is attached to the end of the rode to keep the device submerged. The number of cones and diameter of the rode depends on the displacement of the vessel. With the series drogue deployed from the stern, boat speed will be reduced to not much more than 1 knot, and the risk of excessive yawing and broaching will be all but eliminated. Much like the para-anchor, the series drogue is a passive device. Once deployed there'll be little need for further involvement from the crew who'll be able to batten down the boat and retreat below until conditions improve. Providing Jordan's instructions are closely followed, a series drogue can be homemade by anyone with a sewing machine – and lots of spare time.

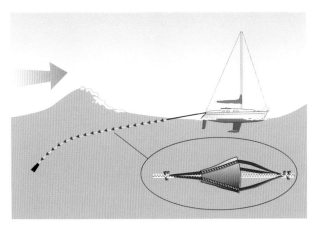

Fig.19.3

The action of a series drogue is relatively gentle once deployed but they need stowing carefully to avoid tangles

Low-pull drogues will slow down the boat to a much lesser extent – typically limiting boat speed to around 4 to 6 knots, which enables the helmsman to steer the boat, at least to a degree. One of the benefits of the low-pull drogue is that it can be used effectively in situations other than extreme conditions. For example a speed-limiting drogue can turn a roller-coaster downwind ride into an easy, subdued sail without adding much to your passage time, as would a medium-pull device.

Just the thing in boisterous trades when sleeping is next to impossible. A speed-limiting drogue will usually be constructed of heavy canvas or webbing, and is deployed on either a bridle or, if increased steering ability is required from the quarter, on a single rode. Much research has gone into the design of drogues of this type, much of it developed from the design of devices used to slow down space re-entry capsules and bringing expensive jet fighters to a stop before they reach the end of the runway. Consequently you shouldn't be tempted to make one yourself – the odds are it will let you down when it really matters.

A drogue should be deployed at more than a full wave period astern. In fact the further astern the better!

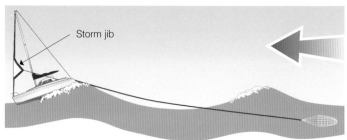

Fig.19.4 Running before a storm

A Further Note of Caution

It's an oft-repeated statistic that more sailors are lost when dinghying back from shoreside than when on an offshore passage. And while this is sadly true, it isn't so widely understood that there's an increased risk in anchorages subject to offshore winds, as is almost always the case in the Caribbean. With most anchorages on the leeward side of the islands, engine failure could mean being driven rapidly offshore in the brisk north-easterly trade winds. Without water or shelter, and with your next landfall several hundred miles away on the coast of Venezuela, the odds of survival aren't in your favour. Tragically, local fishermen are lost this way far too frequently.

As well as wearing lifejackets or buoyancy aids and clipping on the engine killcord, which you should always do, standard dinghy equipment should include:

- An anchor and plenty of rode
- A bailer
- Oars and a seat
- A hand-held VHF radio
- Flares
- Drinking water

PLANNING & STRATEGY

The increasing number of yachts that cross the Atlantic each year could lead you to conclude that this once formidable undertaking is now a piece of cake. You'd be wrong. It takes just as much planning and resourcefulness as it always did, and finding an adequate time slot for it in our increasingly complicated lives is probably more difficult than ever.

There's little doubt that the success of the Atlantic Rally for Cruisers (ARC) has contributed greatly to this growing trend. This annual event draws upwards of two hundred yachts from all over Europe to a starting point in the Canary Islands in late November, aiming to get all entrants across in time for Christmas in the Caribbean. Great emphasis is put on safety. A series of seminars and training courses are organised to help skippers and crews prepare for the rally, and on passage daily position reporting and radio communication is a mandatory requirement. By the time the crews set off on passage for St Lucia much of the trepidation associated with 'being out there on your own' has been largely abated.

The Atlantic Ocean has seasonal weather conditions and surface currents would seem to have been designed for an annual clockwise circuit under sail. A boat leaving the UK in July could take a leisurely summer cruise down through France, Spain and Portugal. In the autumn the passage to Madeira and onward to the Canary Islands could be made, in time for setting off on the trade wind crossing in the early winter months. Alternatively, continue south to the Cape Verdes, and make the crossing from there to Brazil, cruising this coastline before sailing onward to Trinidad or Barbados.

A yacht arriving in Barbados should then have a great downwind romp to Grenada at the southern end of the Caribbean island chain. Late winter and spring will see the yacht heading north through these wonderful islands – Carriacou, Union Island, Mayreau and the Tobago Cays, Canouan, Mustique, Bequia, St Vincent, St Lucia, Martinique, Dominica, Guadeloupe – arriving in either Antigua or St Martin ready for the start of the passage home in May, well before the start of the hurricane season. Setting out northwards towards Bermuda will get you to the Gulf Stream and the favourable winds of the Atlantic high-pressure system which should whisk you across to the Azores, from where you'll pick up the North Atlantic Drift and the prevailing south-westerly winds, which will drive you onwards to the UK to arrive in time for the Wimbledon singles finals.

But only a lucky few can organise their lives such that a full year can be dedicated to an Atlantic circuit. Many choose to break it up into its component parts – the summer passage south, the offshore passages to the Canary Islands and maybe the Cape Verdes, the trade-wind crossing, the Caribbean cruise through the island chain, and finally the return crossing to the Azores and the passage home to the UK – and may take several years to do it, flying back to the UK as other commitments demand.

Like all travellers, we cruisers are occasionally exposed to health risks that we're not accustomed to in the UK. As the mysterious 'they' say, prevention is better than cure.

Staying Healthy

Your first port of call should be at www.masta-travel-health.com. This is the website of the Medical Advisory Service for Travellers Abroad (MASTA) from where you'll be able to purchase, for the price of a sandwich, a travel health brief customised for all the countries you intend to visit on your voyage. Your health brief will provide information on:

- Recommended vaccinations
- Seasonal diseases
- Malaria advice
- The latest travel health news
- Foreign Office travel advice

Apart from the Dominican Republic, where malaria remains a very real risk, this disease has been eradicated from the West Indies. Nevertheless, we keep anti-malarial tablets onboard, but they are only effective for a specific strain of the disease. It's therefore important that if you are going to get bitten by a mosquito, you get bitten by the right one. Apparently it's only the female mosquitoes that bite, the male ones being content to terrorise you with their high-pitched whine.

Dengue fever is prevalent throughout the Windward Islands, but there's nothing that can be taken to reduce the effects of this debilitating mosquito-borne disease. Just use repellent when the little blighters are about – and be lucky.

Next, navigate your way to www.ehic.org, where you'll be able to complete an online application form for a European Health Insurance Card (EHIC). This is the replacement for the no longer valid E111 Form and can be used to cover any necessary medical treatment due to either an accident or illness within the European Economic Community (EEC) and entitles the holder to state-provided medical treatment within the country they are visiting.

The really good news is that the EHIC is valid in the Portuguese islands of Madeira and the Azores, and the French Caribbean islands of Martinique, Guadeloupe, St Martin and St Barts. In these islands you'll be entitled to emergency medical treatment on the same terms as the nationals of those countries, but not for repatriation to the UK. For that you will need a personal Health Insurance Policy tailored for the requirements of cruising abroad. A good place to start your enquiries is with your yacht insurance company.

Yacht Insurance

Here, the devil is most definitely in the detail. If the level of cover isn't expressed in clear and concise terms, don't sign it until you're absolutely sure of uncovered risks. It's always good to ask the 'What if …?' type questions to your insurance company. Recently a pal of mine had his boat eaten from the inside out by an infestation of termites while stored ashore in St Lucia. I asked my insurers if, had it happened to *Alacazam*, I'd have been covered.

"No," they said. "You'd be alright with rats, but termites no."

The two main issues, infestations of malicious insects excepted, will be the policy requirements concerning crew levels for the crossing, and the hurricane clause if you intend to leave your yacht in the Caribbean during the summer months. Some insurance policies insist on a minimum crew of three people for the crossing, which may not suit your plans. Others will provide little or heavily qualified cover for hurricanes and named storms. You just have to shop around.

The Hurricane Season

June, too soon
July, stand by
August, look out you must
September, remember
October, all over.

Or so the ditty goes. Hardly the stuff of the Poet Laureate, but a reasonable guide as to what you can expect.

For each hurricane season, the US National Hurricane Centre (www.nhc.noaa.gov) generates a list of pre-approved names for tropical storms, which is a revolving storm with sustained wind speeds of up to 73mph that may grow up to be a hurricane, and hurricanes. Until 1979 the names were always female but, with the advent of political correctness, the lists now alternate between male and female. The tropical storms and hurricanes are named alphabetically from the list in chronological order. Thus the first one of the year has a name that begins with 'A' and the second is given the name that begins with 'B.' The lists contains names that begin from 'A' to 'W', but exclude names that begin with a 'Q' or 'U'.

The lists of names rotate on a six-yearly cycle and only change when, following a hurricane of particular devastation, the name is retired for at least ten years and another one replaces it. Hence Charley, Frances, Ivan and Jeanne didn't reappear in 2010, Dennis, Katrina and Wilma will sit out 2011 as will Dean, Felix and Noel in 2013.

Hurricanes are categorised from 1 to 5 in increasing ferocity in the Saffir-Simpson Hurricane Wind Scale by their sustained wind speeds at surface level:

Category 1	74 to 95mph
Category 2	96 to 110mph
Category 3	111 to 130mph
Category 4	131 to 155mph
Category 5	>155mph

My personal strategy in managing hurricanes is to be a long way away from the area in which they're likely to occur during the hurricane season.

This resulted in my anxious internet tracking of Ivan in 2004, which battered *Alacazam* while she was laid-up ashore in Grenada.

Fortunately hurricanes grow relatively slowly from humble origins – they're first detected as a tropical wave before developing into a tropical depression, and then going on to a tropical storm – and may fizzle out at any stage. This means that forecasters are able to give us good warning of their development – but only an educated guess as to what direction they're likely to head off in.

Weather Tactics

From the Canary Islands the traditional advice is to sail south until the butter melts and then turn right. Refrigeration has put paid to this technique, and modern thinking suggests 25°N, 25°W as being the point at which the trade winds become properly established.

Marine weather forecasts tend to be fairly reliable for 3 to 4 days ahead, but diminishingly so after that. This is fine for the passages out to the Canary Islands, but they're of limited value once you've released your lines and set out on the 3,000-odd mile passage to the West Indies. You'll have got good four-day forecasts from www.weatheronline.com and the American Navy site at www.fnmoc.navy.mil and NAVTEX will get you weather information from the Las Palmas station for the first few days at sea, after which you'll be out of range and will have to interpret weatherfax charts, assuming you've got SSB and the necessary software.

Unless that is, you enlist with Herb Hillgenberg's net (call sign GX498 but more commonly known as 'Southbound II') on 12359kHz from 2000hrs. Herb operates out of Ontario, Canada and is a highly regarded amateur forecaster who specialises in giving free route forecasting to sailing vessels crossing the Atlantic.

Even if you choose not to enlist, much can be learned by eavesdropping, particularly if he's giving routing information to a yacht close to your position.

Another useful service is provided by the 'Transatlantic Mobile Maritime Net' run by Trudi (callsign 8P6QM) in Barbados. Trudi broadcasts on 21400kHz at 1300hrs each day and gives an English translation of the daily French forecast, which is the only one I know of that covers the crossing. Yachts also check in with her and give their positions and prevailing weather conditions.

Watchkeeping

Some crews on an ocean passage just turn in when it gets dark and resume a watch-keeping system at dawn. This a dangerous practice and, being in breach of Rule 17 of the International Regulations for the Prevention of Collisions at Sea, which requires that a lookout be kept at all times, is technically illegal. They may argue that, having set up warning zones on the radar, a watch is being kept, but this is a bit tenuous in my view. For a crew of two, a good watch-keeping rota is two six-hour watches during daylight hours and three four-hour watches at night. This means that during one 24-hour period one person (person A) does two four-hour night watches and one six-hour day watch, and the other (person B) does one four-hour night watch and one six-hour day watch. In the following 24-hour period person B does two night watches and one day watch and person A does one night watch and one day watch. It's a tiring regime, but it works.

	12 hrs Daylight		12 hrs Darkness			
	0800 - 1400	1400 - 2000	2000 - 2400	0000 - 0400	0400 - 0800	0800 -
Watchkeeper A	✓		✓		✓	
Watchkeeper B		✓		✓		✓

Fig. 20.1   ... and so on

21

... & FINALLY

The end of an Atlantic crossing. Yacht safely anchored in a blissful Caribbean anchorage. Time for your first run ashore. You've made it – but you haven't yet arrived. To be able to say that, you must first check in with Customs & Immigration and then go through a similar process when it's time to move on.

Clearing In and Out

Unlike the countries of the European Community, with their now rather casual approach to international borders, customs and immigration procedures here are taken very seriously. A considerable amount of form filling is involved, together with a close examination of passports, insurance documents and boat registration papers. Customs & Immigration officials will be smartly dressed – long trousers and crisp white shirts are the norm. While the same high standard is not expected of you, it's disrespectful to pitch up in a tatty old pair of shorts and a sleeveless vest – and rightly so. Apart from the French islands, all Customs & Immigration offices have a television. It's there for one reason – cricket. If a game is on, you shouldn't expect to be the centre of attention. If the West Indies are playing, it may be some time before your presence is noticed at all. It helps if you know something about the game, and can offer an intelligent comment, although it may well be a mistake to chortle gleefully if someone is beating the West Indies. Your patience and courtesy will be richly rewarded – "Welcome to the West Indies, Captain." Evening approaches. Yachts rock gently to their anchors as the sun slips inexorably towards the horizon.

Rules and regulations for clearance vary from country to country. Make sure that you follow them according to where your boat is registered. For more information, see http://www.rya.org.uk/cruising/Pages/default.aspx.

The Green Flash

Just before the sun disappears below the horizon, the final sector of it sometimes appears to turn bright green. There is a scientific explanation for it in which words like refraction, dispersion and retinal bleaching turn up. Had I paid more attention to my physics master all those years ago, I would be able to understand the phenomena. But it does happen. I've seen it. Not the lighting up of half the sky as I was foolishly expecting, but just a glimmer for a second or so.

Darkness approaches swiftly, and it will stay that way for nearly 12 hours. If only we could have the long summer days of northern latitudes down here in the tropics – it would be perfect. But just as it is, it comes close.

Journey's end... for now!

APPENDIX

Risk Register

In chapter 18, reference was made to Risk Registers, a useful technique which can be adopted to assess the significance of gear failures on your boat. It comprises a list of all the things that could fail – and will inevitably be a long one!

You'll find it convenient to group the various items under broader headings – sails, rigging, engine, deck gear, domestic, etc. – and rationalise them into sub-groups before moving on to the next step.

Evaluate each item on the list in terms of its:

- Probability of occurrence, rated as low (very unlikely to happen), medium (a fair chance of this happening) or high (almost a certainty), and
- Impact, similarly rated as low (not important, won't affect much if it happens), medium (this would need fixing) or high (a serious problem, could curtail the voyage).

You'll now be able to categorise each risk as to its overall severity, combining probability and impact, where:

- A Category 1 risk (High Probability/High Impact) represents an unacceptable risk event – the ultimate 'show-stopper'. If you have one of these in your risk register you shouldn't go to sea before taking measures as necessary to reduce either its probability of occurrence or its impact – or both. To take a rather daft example, if you only have one winch handle aboard the odds are you'll lose it over the side at some stage – a high probability – and its loss would have a high impact. Clearly you need a couple of spares.
- Category 2 to 6 risks represent manageable risk events in diminishing levels of severity.
- Category 7 risks (Low Probability/Low Impact) represent an inconsequential risk event which could be tolerated.

In assessing 'probability of occurrence', the age and condition of the parts associated with the risk event will to a large extent decide how you rate it, as will the duration of your intended voyage.

Clearly, if your standing rigging is new, the risk of shroud failure will be lower than if it was 10 or 12 years old. In this latter situation, a prudent skipper planning an ocean crossing may well decide to mitigate the risk by replacing some or all of it. Even so, he's still likely to carry a few short lengths of appropriately sized rigging wire, together with bulldog grips, shackles, cringles and Sta-Lok (or Norseman) terminals. Similarly, in assessing 'impact', circumstances will affect the rating. A shroud failure will be rated 'high' wherever and whenever it occurs, but a toilet pump failure on a channel crossing will have much less of an impact for a single-hander than for a fully crewed yacht halfway across the Pacific.

Having gone through this analysis you can now apply a degree of objectivity to what spares you should carry on board. Obviously all 'High Risk' items (Categories 1 to 3) must be catered for in depth, as these will be the ones that would seriously affect your progress and safety on the voyage, whereas you may feel that fewer spares are required for 'Medium Risk' items (Categories 4 and 5), and maybe none at all for 'Low Risk' items (Categories 6 and 7), these being minor inconveniences that could be lived with until your arrival in port.

Probability and Impact Score Sheet

Probability of Occurrence	Probability rating	Impact	Impact Rating	Total Rating
High	3	High	5	8
High	3	Medium	3	6
High	3	Low	1	4
Medium	2	High	5	7
Medium	2	Medium	3	5
Medium	2	Low	1	3
Low	1	High	5	6

Risks are evaluated in terms of two considerations – the **probability** of the anticipated risk occurring, and the impact it would have if it did. Each of these attracts a score to provide a numerical evaluation of each total risk, as follows:

1. **Probability of occurrence,** rated as low (score 1, very unlikely to happen), medium (score 2, a fair chance of this happening) or high (score 3, almost a certainty), and

2. **Impact,** similarly rated as low (score 1, not important, won't affect much if it happens), medium (score 3, this would need fixing) or high (score 5, a serious problem, could curtail the voyage).

The score sheet above shows how the scores are aggregated to evaluate a high risk (high probability + high impact) diminishing to a low risk (low probability + low impact).

Risk Category Table (derived from Probability and Impact Score Sheet)

Probability of Occurrence	Probability rating	Impact	Impact Rating	Total Rating	Risk Rating	
High	3	High	5	8	1	Very High
Medium	2	High	5	7	2	High
High	3	Medium	3	6	3	High
Low	1	High	5	6	3	High
Medium	2	Medium	3	5	4	Medium
High	3	Low	1	4	5	Medium
Low	1	Medium	3	4	5	Medium
Medium	2	Low	1	3	6	Low
Low	1	Low	1	2	7	Low

Here the Probability and Impact score sheet has been sorted in descending order of risk rating which enables the risks to be categorised between very high and low.

Clearly a 'Very High' risk is unacceptable. Some means of mitigating the risk and reducing its category must be found.

Similarly, you won't rest easy if you haven't done anything about the 'High' risks, but you may feel that the medium and low risks are, to a greater or lesser extent, manageable.

What follows is the Risk Register itself. Although the details are typical, they may not accord with the risks on any particular boat and should not be regarded as definitive. It is very important that you make your own evaluation of your own boat and develop a register that fits the specific circumstances.

	Probability			Impact			Risk Category
	High	Med	Low	High	Med	Low	
Sails and rigging							
Halyard breaks		✓		✓			2
Sail rips		✓		✓			2
Reefing line fails		✓			✓		3
Rigging screw fails			✓	✓			3
Shroud breaks			✓	✓			3
Furling gear jams			✓	✓			3
Power supply							
Fuse blows in solar/wind charge regulator		✓		✓			2
Wind generator loses a blade		✓			✓		3
Engine alternator fails			✓		✓		4
Engine							
Alternator drive belt breaks		✓		✓			2
Cooling water belt fails		✓		✓			2
Cooling water impellor fails		✓		✓			2
Watermaker fails		✓		✓			2
Fridge compressor belt fails		✓				✓	4
Electronics							
Autopilot fails		✓		✓			2
Wind anemometer fails		✓				✓	4
VHF won't transmit/receive			✓	✓			3
GPS fails			✓		✓		4
Navigation light fails		✓		✓			2
Electric bilge pump fails			✓		✓		4
Domestic							
Toilet fails to pump		✓		✓			2
Galley foot/hand pump fails			✓	✓			3
Gas supply failure			✓	✓			3
Deck gear							
Windvane servo blade is damaged		✓		✓			2
Winch handle loss		✓		✓			2
Manual bilge pump fails			✓	✓			3
Wheel steering cable breaks			✓	✓			3
Winch seizes			✓	✓			3
Windvane blade is lost			✓	✓			3
Deck hatch leaks			✓		✓		4
Turning block fails			✓		✓		4

Having carried out your risk assessment, your spares list may look something like this:

- Spare alternator
- Alternator diodes
- Voltage regulator for solar panels
- Voltage regulator for wind generator
- Bulbs and fuses for all electric appliances
- Circuit breakers
- Electric wiring of various sizes
- Spare electrical terminals and connectors
- Spare fuel pump
- Spare raw water pump
- Spare injectors
- Spare V belts
- Spare engine oil filters and primary and secondary fuel filters
- Service kit for the watermaker and plenty of spare filters
- Spare cooling water impellers and impeller replacement kits
- Service kit for sea toilet
- Spare seals for each deck hatch
- Service kit for all manual pumps
- Spare electric bilge pump
- Pressure regulator for gas bottle
- Service kit for sheet and halyard winches
- Spare winch handles
- Shackles of various types and sizes
- Replacement blocks and jammers for the mainsheet tackle and kicker
- Assorted blocks including a couple of snatch blocks
- Assorted clevis pins and split pins
- Stainless steel nuts, bolts and washers of various lengths and diameters

- Assorted stainless steel self-tapping screws
- Sail repair kit including sail cloth
- Spare sail battens
- Sail slides and jib hanks
- Turnbuckles and toggles
- Spare sheets and halyards
- Assorted ropes and cordage
- Norseman fitting for each shroud diameter
- Spare bottle screws for each shroud diameter
- Spare windex
- Emergency VHF antenna
- Handheld GPS (as backup to fixed unit)
- Handheld VHF (as backup to fixed unit)
- Handheld compass with bulkhead clip (as backup to main steering compass)
- Spare batteries for torches and electronic devices
- Fibreglass repair kit, including mat, cloth resin and underwater epoxy
- Emergency tiller
- Spare blade for wind generator
- Hose clamps and lengths of hose
- Spare servo pendulum blade for self-steering
- Spare windvane for self-steering
- Spare air cylinders for foghorn
- Various connectors for shoreside power supplies
- Dinghy repair kit
- Sheer pins for outboard motor propeller
- Spark plugs for outboard motor

Tools

You will need tools to make any repairs. These should include:

- Socket set
- Spanner set
- Allen keys
- Filter wrench
- Large and small adjustable spanner
- Pliers of various types and sizes
- Metal files
- Hacksaw and spare blades
- Parallel punches
- Claw hammer
- Ball peen hammer
- Club hammer
- Mallet
- Tape measure
- 12v cordless drill with assorted bits

- Screwdrivers of various types and sizes
- 12v inverter
- Set of fids
- Marlin spike
- Rigger's knife
- Sailmaker's palm and assorted needles
- Sewing machine (Reeds Sailmaker or similar)
- Wire cutters and strippers
- Gas torch with soldering attachment
- Set of feeler gauges
- Large magnet
- Small plane
- Wood chisels
- Whetstone

Don't forget any specialist tools you may need. For example, you may need to carry a special socket to remove the recessed nut on a folding propeller.

Electrical tools

- Multimeter – preferably digital
- Needle nose pliers
- Crimping tools
- Small screwdrivers
- Side cutters
- Polarity tester
- Wire strippers
- Test light
- Butane soldering iron

Fishing Tackle

You don't need any fancy equipment to catch a few fish for the galley. Nor do you need to make the endeavour an all-consuming activity. A simple handline correctly rigged, trolled astern and left to its own devices will produce the goods. Just check the lure now and again to remove any detritus it may have picked up.

Here's what you need:

- An offshore trolling handline, or ideally two. You'll double your chances of success if you set one from each quarter. Have a look on my website at www.go-saltwater-fishing.com/handline-fishing.html for details of how to put it all together
- A selection of trolling lures – plastic squid lures, skirted lures (and spare skirts), plugs and spoons
- Small oval sinkers to insert into the heads of the plastic squid lures
- Lead trolling weights to get the lure below the surface
- Spare hooks and stainless steel split rings for each lure
- A hook-sharpening file
- A spool of 300lb breaking strain nylon monofilament fishing line for making up leaders
- A crimping tool and double-barrelled crimps to suit 300lb line

- Swivels and snaps with a breaking strain of not less than 300lb. Ball bearing swivels are best
- Bungee cord to make up a snubber, details of which are on my website
- Tough gloves to protect your hands when hauling in your catch
- A gaff to boat your catch; make sure it's long enough to reach it
- A hook removal tool (or long-nose pliers) to get the hook out safely
- Appropriate knives for cleaning and filleting the fish
- A cut-proof filleting glove to protect the hand that isn't operating your super-sharp filleting knife
- A fish scaling tool
- Stout scissors for removing fins
- A tackle box to stow your gear
- A good fish recipe book

INDEX

Notes

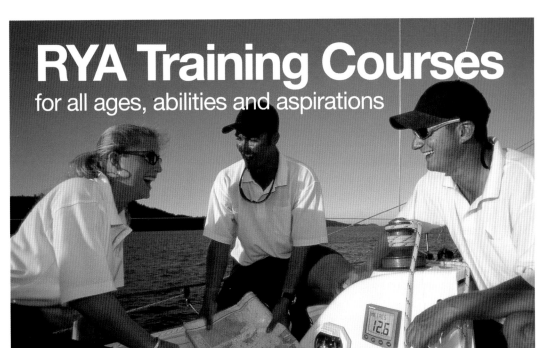

Promoting and Protecting Boating

The RYA is the national organisation which represents the interests of everyone who goes boating for pleasure. The greater the membership, the louder our voice when it comes to protecting members' interests. Apply for membership today, and support the RYA, to help the RYA support you.

Benefits of Membership

- Special members' discounts on a range of products and services including boat insurance, books, charts, DVDs and class certificates
- Access to expert advice on all aspects of boating from legal wrangles to training matters
- Free issue of Certificate of Competence; increasingly asked for by overseas governments, holiday companies, insurance underwriters and boat hire companies

- Third Party insurance for windsurfing members
- Access to the wide range of RYA publications, including the RYA quarterly magazine
- E-newsletters, tailored to the type of boating you enjoy, to keep you up to date and give you the chance to join the debate on issues that affect you
- Regular offers in RYA Magazine
- ...and much more

JOIN NOW

Membership form opposite or join online at www.rya.org.uk

Visit our website for information, advice, members' services and web shop.

IT'S ALL ABOUT YOU

AND THE BOATING YOU DO

RYA MEMBERSHIP APPLICATION

Be part of it

One of boating's biggest attractions is its freedom from rules and regulations. As an RYA member you'll play an active part in keeping it that way, as well as benefiting from free expert advice and information, plus discounts on a wide range of boating products, charts and publications.

To join the RYA, please complete the application form below and send it to The Membership Department, RYA, RYA House, Ensign Way, Hamble, Southampton, Hampshire SO31 4YA. You can also join online at www.rya.org.uk, or by phoning the membership department on +44 (0) 23 8060 4159. Whichever way you choose to apply, you can save money by paying by Direct Debit. A Direct Debit instruction is on the back of this form.

	Title	Forename	Surname	Gender	Date of Birth
Applicant ❶					/ /
Applicant ❷					/ /
Applicant ❸					/ /
Applicant ❹					/ /

Address

Post Code

E-mail Applicant ❶

E-mail Applicant ❷

E-mail Applicant ❸

E-mail Applicant ❹

Home Tel   Day Time Tel   Mobile Tel

Type of membership required (Tick Box) – Annual Rate

Junior (0-11)	£5 by direct debit	£5 non direct debit rate	
Youth (12-17)	£10 by direct debit	£15 non direct debit rate	
Under 25	£20 by direct debit	£25 non direct debit rate	
Personal	£40 by direct debit	£45 non direct debit rate	
Family*	£60 by direct debit	£65 non direct debit rate	

Save money by completing the Direct Debit form overleaf

Please number up to three boating interests in order, with number one being your principal interest

Yacht Cruising	Dinghy Racing	Dinghy Cruising
Personal Watercraft	Sportboats & RIBs	Motor Boating
Powerboat Racing	Windsurfing	
	Canal Cruising	River Cruising

* Family Membership: 2 adults plus any under 18s all living at the same address. Prices valid until 30/9/2013. One discount voucher is accepted for individual memberships, and two discount vouchers are accepted for family membership.

IMPORTANT In order to provide you with membership benefits the details provided by you on this form and in the course of your membership will be maintained on a database. If you do not wish to receive information on member services and benefits please tick here ☐. By applying for membership of the RYA you agree to be bound by the RYA's standard terms and conditions (copies on request or at www.rya.org.uk)

Signature   Date   /   /

Source Code   0 7 7

Joining Point Code

RYA
Be part of it

GET MORE FROM
YOUR
BOATING
SUPPORT THE
RYA

PAY BY DIRECT DEBIT – AND SAVE MONEY

Instructions to your Bank or Building Society to pay by Direct Debit

Please fill in the form and send to:
Membership Department, Royal Yachting Association, RYA House, Ensign Way, Hamble,
Southampton, Hampshire SO31 4YA.

Name and full postal address of your Bank/Building Society

To the Manager   Bank/Building Society

Address

Postcode

Name(s) of Account Holder(s)

Branch Sort Code

Bank/Building Society Account Number

DIRECT Debit

Originator's Identification Number

9	5	5	2	1	3

RYA Membership Number (For office use only)

Instructions to your Bank or Building Society

Please pay Royal Yachting Association Direct Debits from the account detailed in
this instruction subject to the safeguards assured by The Direct Debit Guarantee.
I understand that this instruction may remain with the Royal Yachting Association
and, if so, details will be passed electronically to my Bank/Building Society.

Signature(s)

Date: D D / M M / Y Y Y Y